The Urban Challenge

THE URBAN CHALLENGE

EDITORS:
Larry L. Rose
C. Kirk Hadaway

BROADMAN PRESS
Nashville, Tennessee

© Copyright 1982 ● BROADMAN PRESS
All rights reserved.
4262-38

ISBN: 0-8054-6238-4
Dewey Decimal Classification: 254.22
Subject Heading: CITY CHURCHES

Library of Congress Catalog Card Number: 82-71026
Printed in the United States of America

Unless otherwise noted, Scripture quotations are from the King James Version of the Bible. Scripture quotations marked RSV are from the Revised Standard Version of the Bible, copyright 1946, 1952, © 1971, 1973. Scripture quotations marked NASB are from the *New American Standard Bible*. Copyright © The Lockman Foundation, 1960, 1962, 1963, 1971, 1972, 1973, 1975. Used by permission.
Scripture quotations marked NEB are from *The New English Bible*. Copyright © The Delegates of the Oxford University Press, 1961, 1970. Reprinted by permission.

Preface

With the rapid urbanization of the world and the growing interdependence of nations, churches in America must be aware of the world around them. Indeed, the United States and most of the industrialized nations of the world are already urban societies and many Third World countries are moving in this direction. Our cities are not growing as fast as in previous years. Nevertheless, the metropolitan regions of our nation still contain the bulk of the United States population, and many have still not recovered from the convulsive growth of the past. Downtown areas have decayed through neglect; inner cities are still choked with slums or gutted through "urban renewal"; neighborhoods are aging; and suburban sprawl has created a disordered, congested landscape.

In the midst of the city with all its problems, churches still seek to minister. How they do so is the subject of this book. We hope these chapters will speak to those involved in urban ministry because churches have not always been successful nor always spiritually authentic in their approach to the peoples of the city. Too often churches have seemed at the mercy of the city rather than being positive influences and prophetic voices. Our churches have grown or declined along with the population, embodied a "culture religion," and have failed to minister cross-culturally. When faced with difficult situations, too often churches have taken the easy way out rather than facing the changes that life in the city inevitably brings.

But all is not bleak. Cities across America are beginning to cope with their problems and lack of identity. People are discovering that cities *can* be good places to live and work. Neighborhood change has slowed and given community organizations, including the church, time to adapt.

It is possible for churches to understand urbanization and the changes it brings. By doing so, they can act before problems become critical. Many models of effective urban ministry are emerging in our day and can be used to reach new populations with the gospel. Strategies can be created so individual churches do not have to go it alone, and the city can become a place of possibilities rather than a place of problems.

We are embarking on a new adventure in our society, one that not only offers great technological advances but also has many diverse problems. Churches have never before had a greater opportunity to communicate the gospel. Yet, with all the technological apparatus available, the churches would do well to remember that the Christian faith and message are personal, and there never will be a substitute for close human relationships.

In the local community church individuals can and should be able to find the family of God in its fullest expression of the Father. It is our desire that this book be of assistance to those involved in the spreading of the good news of the kingdom.

LARRY L. ROSE
C. KIRK HADAWAY
October 1982
Nashville, Tennessee

Contents

1
Toward an Urban Awareness
Larry L. Rose and C. Kirk Hadaway

The United States has long been an urban nation. As in other industrialized countries of the world, our cities have been magnets, drawing people from the rural hinterlands and, in some eras, from overseas. The 1980 census revealed that three fourths of the United States population live in metropolitan centers, and many more live in smaller cities and towns.[1] The domination of American culture by the cities of this land has been a fact of life for years, but has the church in America come to grips with this reality? We think it has not.

Religious denominations in America developed in a rural nation and many, if not most, are still rural oriented with a distrust of cities and a view of them as places which hold nothing but problems for Christian ministry. To a large extent, this view only mirrors our national ambivalence to the city. As one urban planner and developer put it, "We have lived so long with grim, congested, worn-out inner cities and sprawling, cluttered outer cities, that we have subconsciously come to accept them as inevitable and unavoidable. Deep down in our national heart is a lack of conviction that cities can be beautiful, humane, and truly responsive to the needs and yearnings of our people."[2]

The negative image which many cities in America have gained tends to mask their resources, power, and influence. It is in Washington, D.C., New York City, Chicago, Los Angeles, San Francisco, and other "world-class" cities that the political power of the nation is controlled, as is international trade, the national communication networks, and economic exchange. Such cities reflect the vitality of the nation and greatly influence its prosperity or lack thereof.

What Is Urban?

The first census taken in 1790 showed that more than 95 percent of the population of the United States lived in rural areas and only 5 percent in urban areas.[3] This overwhelming ruralness becomes even more apparent when it is realized that any town or village with a population of 2,500 or more was considered urban.

Today around 75 percent of the American public lives in metropolitan areas. So it is clear that our previous ruralness is a thing of the past. But what does *metropolitan* actually mean? The terms *metropolitan* and *urban* are typically used interchangeably to refer to large cities, but each has a very distinct meaning as defined by the United States Census Bureau. Metropolitan areas, for instance, refer to Standard Metropolitan Statistical Areas. SMSAs, as they are called, are composed of one or more counties (or townships in New England) and must include at least 50,000 persons in a central city or urbanized area. There are presently 323 SMSAs in the United States, the largest of which is New York City, with a total population of 9,119,737.[4] The boundaries of SMSAs are typically drawn rather widely, so some areas included may not seem very urban. However, areas are only included if they are "metropolitan in character" and are highly integrated with the central city. In practical terms, this means the population must be predominantly nonagricultural in occupation and contain a sizable work force with substantial numbers employed in the central cities. Such counties thus only appear somewhat rural; in reality they are an integral part of the metropolitan community.

The meaning of *urban*, as defined by the Census Bureau is quite distinct from that of *metropolitan*, even though the percent of Americans living in urban areas is nearly identical to the percent living in metropolitan areas. To be called *urban* an area must be within a city or town (place) with a minimum population of 2,500 or be an area surrounding an urban center which meets some minimum population density requirements.[5] Because of this definition, some towns which would seem hardly urban are included and some suburban and exurban territories surrounding very large cities would be excluded.

In this book, we will employ the metropolitan definition because it excludes relatively small, isolated cities and towns. We will continue to use the term *urban*, however, because it is more familiar than *metropolitan*. But when an actual percentage figure is used such as percent urban or percent metropolitan the strict census definitions will be employed.

Urbanization and the Church

The trend toward urbanization began in earnest shortly after the end of the Civil War and by 1920 the United States had increased to 51 percent urban.[6] But Protestant denominations in America have not kept up with the rapid pace of urbanization. For instance, the Southern Baptist Convention, which is the largest American Protestant body with nearly 14 million members, has only 38 percent of its churches in metropolitan areas.[7] This compares to 75 percent of the American public which resides in these same metropolitan communities. It might be thought that this only results from the fact that 85 percent of Southern Baptists live in the South, which is more rural than the nation as a whole. But recent statistics show that Southern Baptists are much *less* concentrated in metropolitan areas than even the general population of the South.[8]

As we see it, the problem of the church and its ambivalent attitude toward the city has two main roots. The first is one of an inherently conservative institution failing to adjust to change, and the second is a broader societal problem: the sorry state of the large city in America. In viewing both the development of the church in the city and the city itself, it is helpful to divide the history of the United States into a series of eras or "societies."

The United States began as an agrarian or agricultural society which continued until about the 1860s. Villages and the few cities that existed acted as centers of market and trade rather than manufacturing. The agrarian society was rural oriented, localistic, and in many ways very traditional. In this era, our modern denominations emerged, and the traditionally irreligious American public finally became largely "churched." From the founding of the American colonies, only a very small proportion of the population was on the membership rolls of colonial churches. The churches were, by and large, somewhat elitist and quite exclusionary. Modern Christians tend to have an overly idealistic impression of our founding fathers and forget that many Revolutionary leaders had extremely unorthodox theological views and that the general public was quite apathetic toward the church.[9] Settlers had expanded outward from the seaboard and had not taken the church with them.

The situation changed drastically, however, through the first and second Great Awakenings. Revivalism spread throughout the sparsely populated states, and new churches were spawned by the thousands. The result was a vastly different religious landscape. The proportion of church members increased from *only around 6 percent* in 1775 to perhaps *23 percent* by 1842 and *43 percent* by 1910, and denominational strengths underwent a major shuffling.[10] The primary gainers in this period were the Methodists, Baptists, Presbyterians, and Christian churches. While these denominations had their roots in cities and towns of the East, their massive expansion in what was then "the West" produced overwhelmingly rural denominations.

A study of social institutions developed in this era shows that they share a rural, localistic, traditionalistic orientation. They were evolved to serve an agrarian society of small towns and villages, and naturally the institutions tended to reflect the orientation of society itself. The Protestant church was no exception.

The second era in our history has been called the industrial society, and this period spanned the years from approximately 1860 to the 1970s. With the mechanization of industry, factories became the more efficient means of producing goods. The cities rapidly became industrialized and created a tremendous need for labor. The lure of better wages drew more and more people from farms and villages to the cities. Massive immigration from Europe also fueled the growth of American cities, as did the development of mechanized farming techniques. Larger and more efficient farms meant that large quantities of food could be produced by fewer workers.

All these factors led to the convulsive development of cities in

America. Populations of urban centers doubled and tripled in a few decades. New cities were developed out of small towns and grew faster than basic services could be provided. Zoning was largely unheard of, so the cities of America grew by sheer chance with no planning or thought about their future. European cities had long ago developed prestigious urban cores where the wealthier members of society lived, close to the center of commerce. But in America a new pattern emerged in which the inner city became the least desirable place to live. Immigrant groups and the rural poor flooded into the inner city while upwardly mobile persons moved farther out. Perhaps if our cities had developed more gradually this would not have happened. Nevertheless, a new type of city emerged in the United States.

As new housing development occurred farther and farther from the urban core and the middle-class exodus proceeded, the inner city began to decay rapidly. In the words of James Rouse, the suburbs "sucked the blood out of the central cities and left behind some of the urban basket cases we see today."[11] In the worst examples, the city proper is now a sea of low income minorities, with a decaying infrastructure and a poor tax base, surrounded by affluent, incorporated suburban developments which contribute only minimally to the financial well-being of the city.

The industrial society produced other changes as well. American society was increasingly dominated by large industries and trade unions, and even world views were altered. It was an active society concerned with *now* rather than the traditions of the past. How did the church react to the change? Church historians tell us that the Protestant churches in America largely failed to join this industrial society. They distrusted the labor unions and in doing so largely ignored the industrial worker. Still, the mainline denominations managed to grow in the cities by their attachment to the rising middle class. They took the suburbs as their own, and today this is where their major strength lies.[12]

There are strong indications that we are undergoing another broad societal change. The coming of the computer and the rapid advance in technology has changed many structures in our society. Some have called this the coming of a "postindustrial" or an "informational" society. A whole new stratum of "knowledge work-ers" has come into being, constituting a new class of citizens, skilled in data analysis and in the use of abstractions. Entire new industries are being created, and old ones are being altered. One indication of this change is in the composition of the American labor force. In 1954, 35 percent of the labor force of the United States was unionized.[13] By 1980 the proportion had dropped to 21 percent.[14] The increase in blue-collar jobs is lower than for any other occupational classification, except farming, while the ranks of managers, professionals, clerks, and service personnel continue to expand at a rapid pace. The population is becoming better educated, more mobile, and cosmopolitan.

At this point, it is somewhat difficult to know what effect the postindustrial society will have on the church and the city. The level of urbanization continues to rise, but it is doing so much more slowly than in the past. Advances in communications have made the centralization of businesses in large cities less essential. Office parks are now found on the periphery of the city, in addition to downtown, and many companies are finding that smaller cities offer as much as larger metro areas without the high operational costs and taxes and the problems of crowding, massive traffic jams, and so forth.

For the church, this trend toward decentralization may be a boon, since Protestant churches seem more at home in the suburbs and small cities. Still, it should be remembered that Protestant denominations have many thousands of churches in the down-towns, inner cities, and urban neighborhoods of America, and there are still millions of people in these areas. Churches have suffered greatly in recent years as neighborhoods have declined in population and undergone racial transition. The future is uncer-tain, but there appears to be a growing awareness that our cities are worth saving. Baltimore, Boston, and many other cities are at last trying to turn around the tide of urban decay. There have been some notable successes already, but the cities and the churches will have to wait for the final outcome.

One of the causes for imbalance in society is related to the inability of certain larger structures and institutions to change as rapidly as the larger society. The church is one such institution. With the coming of rapid urbanization, change has become one of the few constants. Therefore, it is imperative that the church learn to deal with societal changes. The emerging society in the United States today is very much urban oriented. The United States is becoming populated by people reared in urban areas and very much attuned to the urban life-style. Urbanization, therefore, is one of the great challenges of the church in the 1980s.

Urbanization Worldwide

While this book is concerned with urbanization in the United States, it should be remembered that we are now in a period of unprecedented urbanization worldwide. Population growth which continues at a breakneck speed has been coupled with a rapid redistribution of the population from rural to urban areas. The rapidity of this major shift is shown clearly in Figure 1.

Early in this century, urbanization worldwide was only 15 percent, yet a social historian has called the increase during the 1800s, "the most remarkable social phenomenon" of that century.[15]

According to the most recent figures, and if present trends continue, it is likely that over half the world's population will live in urban areas in AD 2000. At that time at least 3.2 billion people will live in urban areas, a total equal to the entire world's population in 1965.[16]

Urban growth, especially in cities of developing nations, will be immense and is already creating sprawling metropolises choked with slums and belts of misery. The need for housing, food, water, and sanitation is already taxing these cities to the limit, and yet the people keep coming.

This rapid world urbanization will have a dramatic impact on the United States. We are becoming more and more a part of the global community and are greatly influenced by events over which we no longer have any control. The rise of massive cities in the developing world will make the plight of the urban poor around the world more visible and the disparity between the "have" and "have not" nations even more apparent. As a result, we can expect pressures for a radical redistribution of wealth in the world and

FIGURE 1
WORLD URBAN AND RURAL POPULATION

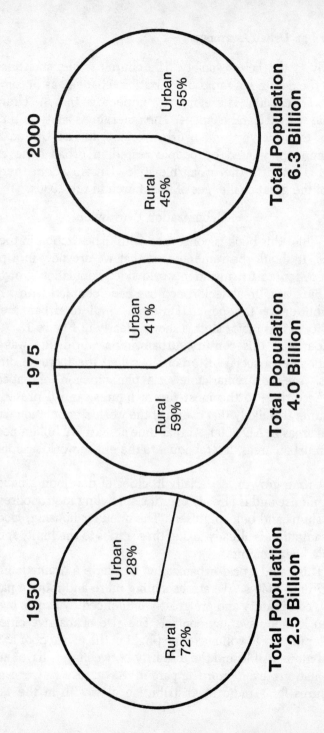

1950 — Rural 72% / Urban 28% — Total Population 2.5 Billion

1975 — Rural 59% / Urban 41% — Total Population 4.0 Billion

2000 — Rural 45% / Urban 55% — Total Population 6.3 Billion

Source: *World Urbanization, 1800 to 2000* (Washington, D.C.: Population Reference Bureau.)

Figure 2

The Ten Most Populous Urban Areas

<u>1975</u>		<u>2000</u>	
New York	19.8	Mexico City	31.0
Tokyo-Yokohama	17.7	Sao Paulo	25.8
Mexico City	11.9	Tokyo-Yokohama	24.2
Shanghai	11.6	New York	22.8
Los Angeles	10.8	Shanghai	22.7
Sao Paulo	10.7	Peking	19.9
London	10.4	Rio de Janeiro	19.0
Greater Bombay	9.3	Greater Bombay	17.1
Rhine-Ruhr	9.3	Calcutta	16.7
Paris	9.2	Djakarta	16.6

Source: United Nations, *Patterns of Urban and Rural Population Growth* (New York: United Nations, 1980).

accelerated pressures from people desiring to emigrate to the United States. Massive legal and illegal immigration will continue. And if harsh legal measures are taken to stem either tide, the image of the United States in the eyes of the Third World will only deteriorate. The world is coming to the United States and taking up residence in American cities. Our "melting pot" is no longer mixing very well, and the churches of America must wake up to an increasing level of cultural diversity.

The Challenge of America's Cities

The intent of this book is to examine issues of urbanization which relate to the church in America. Our desire is to raise the awareness of those involved in the churches to a greater understanding of how to deal with an urbanized society.

The urbanization of the United States and the world calls for churches to become increasingly innovative in their methods. Churches will need to examine new areas and new opportunities for reaching people and be more creative in programming, in style of worship, and in the use of facilities.

With the massive changes brought about by urbanization and the need for churches to respond with innovative approaches, churches will also need *ministers with unique training*. Seminaries will need increasingly to review and revise their curricula and to add programs, courses, and laboratory-type experiences that will relate to the dynamics of urban life. Churches in the 1980s must be willing to accept change, to know that what works today may not work tomorrow. We must continually be willing to evaluate our methodology and be committed to changing that methodology to meet emerging needs.

This book is not the cry that the sky is falling in on the churches, but rather is a plea for churches to use the opportunities that our day brings. Urbanization, along with the increase in population, plus continued immigration to the United States has brought churches in the United States to perhaps their greatest challenge.

Our cities will not be good places to live in if churches and their influence are not presented in an effective way to the people in the cities. It is, therefore, our mandate not to stand on the sidelines and criticize but to become a real catalyst in the cities, to change them, to raise their values and their sense of caring. The challenge of urbanization for churches in the 1980s can be what the challenge of the illegal religion status was to early churches in the first century; for, in spite of the difficulties and adversities, churches grew and expanded their witness into the world.

We have two effective examples in the New Testament of why we should be involved in ministry in the cities. Clearly in the study of the life and ministry of Christ, we see that he spent much of his time and energy in carrying the good news to the people of the cities. One of the passages that exemplifies this is Matthew 11:1: "It came to pass, when Jesus had made an end of commanding his twelve disciples, he departed thence, to teach and preach to their cities."

The apostle Paul is another good example of carrying the gospel to the cities. Numerous times the Scriptures indicate that Paul went to chief cities. One dramatic passage is Acts 16:10-12:

> After he had seen the vision, immediately we endeavoured to go into Macedonia, assuredly gathering that the Lord had called us for to preach the gospel unto them. Therefore loosing from Troas, we came with a straight course to Samothracia, and the next day to Neapolis; and from thence to Philippi, which is the chief city of that part of Macedonia.

Jesus saw the multitudes and had compassion on them, went to them, and shared the good news with them. The mandate of the Great Commission is still the same for our day: see the great multitudes, have compassion, and share with them the good news!

In the following chapters we present a challenge, implications, and suggestions that we hope will encourage you to become involved in the effort to minister and witness to the people of the cities.

In chapter 2, "Understanding American Cities," Paul Geisel looks at the cities through the eyes of a social scientist. He reviews the history and forms of urbanization in the United States and draws implications for churches and denominations. In chapter 3,

"Our Mandate for Reaching Urban America," William Pinson, Jr., deals with the biblical perspective and the mandate of the church to reach urbanites. He paints a graphic portrait of the misery and the excitement of the city. He also shows why we cannot retreat from the task of providing witness and ministry in the urban setting.

The fourth chapter, entitled "The Cultural Captivity of Urban Churches," presents the views of Larry McSwain, a professor of church and community. In his chapter, McSwain deals with cultural factors which necessarily affect all institutions in American society. The church is no exception, and it must first recognize its captivity if it is to become captive instead to a transforming Christ.

In "Our Urban Future," chapter 5, Orrin Morris presents a series of possible futures for the city and church in America. Four visions are given by this professional researcher, each presenting its own challenge to the church of today. The visions range from exciting to somewhat depressing, but each is a future which does not now exist. We create the future by our actions today.

Kirk Hadaway from the Center for Urban Church Studies staff deals with how the local church is affected by its urban environment. In his chapter, "The Church in the Urban Setting," Hadaway looks at both the environment of the church in the city and the structure of the typical neighborhood church in drawing his conclusions. A major emphasis is placed on factors which either encourage or discourage the growth of local congregations.

Dale Cross deals with the problems and possibilities for evangelism in America's cities in chapter 7, "Evangelizing America's Cities." Cross critiques evangelism strategies and presents his own, along with insightful illustrations of effective evangelism as it is happening in cities across America.

Various chapters point to the need for new ways of "doing church" in American cities. In chapter 8, "Alternative Church Models for an Urban Society," Francis DuBose takes on this challenge. Drawing on his vast firsthand experience with churches around the globe, DuBose describes the variety of effective church forms and the reasons each exists. The times demand alternative church models if we are to reach the cities of America and the world.

Don Hammer, Jere Allen, and George Bullard, in "Urban Strategy Through Cooperative Efforts," deal with the need for churches in each city to develop overall strategies for reaching their metropolitan areas. They stress the role of the local association or conference in this process and give as an example a plan called Mega Focus Cities, which is being used by one denomination to develop urban mission strategy at the local level and to concentrate denominational priorities.

Finally, we are joined by G. Willis Bennett of The Southern Baptist Theological Seminary in chapter 10. Here the authors summarize the insights of previous chapters and reemphasize the need for Christians to have an urban awareness and an urban commitment if we are to have any hope of reaching people in the cities for Christ.

The urban challenge is for the urban church, the concerned urban layperson, the urban minister, and the urban missionary. Our purpose is to raise awareness, to challenge, and to help. Judge our success by your own reactions.

Notes

1. Bureau of the Census, *Standard Metropolitan Statistical Areas and Standard Consolidated Statistical Areas: 1980* (Washington, D.C.: U.S. Department of Commerce, 1981), PC80-S1-5, p. 1.

2. Quote from James Rouse in *Time* (Los Angeles: Time Incorporated, August 24, 1981), pp. 44,46.

3. Bureau of the Census, *Historical Statistics of the United States* (Washington, D.C.: U.S. Department of Commerce, 1975), Part 1, p. 12.

4. Bureau of the Census, 1981, p. 47.

5. Bureau of the Census, *County and City Data Book*, 1972 (Washington, D.C.: U.S. Department of Commerce, 1973), p. xxiv, xxxii.

6. Bureau of the Census, 1975, p. 11.

7. C. Kirk Hadaway, "A Compilation of Southern Baptist Churches and Resident Members Located in Standard Metropolitan Statistical Areas, 1978," unpublished paper (Atlanta: Baptist Home Mission Board, 1979), p. 24.

8. C. Kirk Hadaway, "The Fifty Largest Standard Metropolitan Statistical Areas: Southern Baptist Progress, 1970-1980," unpublished paper (Nashville: Center for Urban Church Studies, 1982), p. 2.

9. Martin E. Marty, *Righteous Empire: The Protestant Experience in America* (New York: Harper and Row, 1970), pp. 37-39. Also see Kenneth Scott Latourette, *A History of Christianity* (New York: Harper and Row, 1975), Vol. II, pp. 1045-1046.

10. The earlier figure is based on the number of churches estimated in the colonies. See Winthrop Hudson, *American Protestantism* (Chicago: University of Chicago Press, 1961), p. 4. To obtain the percentage, we used estimates of average congregation size and total population. The 1842 percentage is derived from Robert Baird, *Religion in the United States of America* (Glasgow: Blackie and Son, 1844), pp. 600-649. The latest figure is from Latourette, pp. 1229, 1230. Latourette also estimates the percent in the churches at 6.9 percent in 1800.

11. Rouse, p. 50.

12. Latourette, pp. 1253-1254.

13. Bureau of the Census, 1975, p. 178.

14. *U.S. News and World Report* (Beverly Hills: U.S. News and World Report, Inc., September 14, 1981), p. 63.

15. Adna F. Weber, *The Growth of Cities in the Nineteenth Century* (Ithaca, New York: Cornell University Press, 1963).

16. United Nations, *Patterns of Urban and Rural Population Growth* (New York: United Nations, 1980), p. 11.

2

Understanding American Cities
Paul N. Geisel

Establishment—Change and the American City

The American city is a phenomenon which can only be described in terms of a process. No single historical model exists in any of the centers of population. No single definition of structure, shape, size, or distribution of power can be identified. To a large extent, the only reasonable explanation or description starts with an assumption of constant change. The American city is a dynamic set of interacting systems—political, economic, technological, sociological—which are in constant flux. Institutional structures, by definition, attempt to organize, build for, and manage permanent or at least stable populations. It is extraordinarily difficult for these institutional structures, after years of effort at building systems to respond, to discover that the systems, once in place, are the barriers to resolution in a changing society.

Robert Audrey, author of *The Territorial Imperative*, once remarked that we cannot struggle today as though it were yesterday. This articulates the dilemma since today contains the seed of tomorrow.

Churches, schools, social service agencies, and the like—all resolution institutions in our cities—face the continuing problem that in the process of organizing their resources, building their buildings, developing support bases, and training their personnel they are in the process of becoming passé. If there is anything for us to learn as institutional spokespersons in this latter half of the twentieth century about building and organizing for the American city, it is this expectation and awareness of change.

In a period of a few decades, the American city has undergone tremendous shifts in population composition and in population size. Urban Americans are a mobile people who create and respond to an occupational market. According to the United States Census Bureau's yearly poll, over 45 percent of all Americans moved at least once in the period 1975-1980. For those twenty-five to twenty-nine years of age, 77 percent changed residences in this period. This overwhelming movement of people is reflected in our large cities.

Another part of the paradox of this constantly changing societal system is the fact that our society has inherited so few givens as to how things "should be." We are, while attempting to stabilize as institutional systems, our own force fields for greater and faster change. No urban space starts with an organized church. The church emerges with the community. Congregations and a myriad of services take shape in concert with other institutional systems. As the city grows, a bureaucracy develops to administer as well as to minister. The resource pool of the community also begins to multiply. A small population base can support only one or two persons who are full-time actors. Without belaboring the point, the large city and its large institutions can afford many actors and, indeed, permits and encourages highly specialized skills to emerge. The overall effect of this is to create institutions which can respond with the latest techniques to segments of the community far more rapidly than ever before. The capability, for example, to build and organize for new suburbia is so fast that we create, in some measure, problems for the structures and systems already in place. For example, First Baptist Church of Houston can relocate to an outer area of the city fairly easily. It can maintain its integrity as to type of program and congregational composition. This leaves a vacuum in institutional resource for ministry in the inner city. A new challenge develops. Since Americans as individuals are moving, we in the church are frequently moving with them. The number of inner-city names on suburban buildings is a case in point. This ability to move swiftly accelerates the decline of the inner city.

American cities are unique in that they take the form of their institutional systems. Americans are historically organizers, institution builders. De Toqueville commented over a century and a half ago about this phenomenon of organizing and building. The result is a set of cities that look physically somewhat similar but have unique characters. The differential forms that these structures take become the basis for comparing one city to another. From the church perspective, these differences illustrate that various strategies are possible in advocating our own presence.

A Southern Baptist, for example, finds a church tradition in Boston very different than in Nashville. In order to succeed, real differences in approach must be employed.

This constant change and amazing ability to change, with all the costs, chaos, and confusion, puts the American city on the world stage. Our cities are European-appearing but are not European. Our cities are made up of greatly divergent ethnic groups, religious groups, political positions, and so forth. The world views us with some fascination. We are not loved or hated, but we do have their attention because in large part we are "downtown to the world." Every racial group, every income group, looks to the American city as where life is happening. We have crime, riots, social isolation, loneliness, ghettos, and the poor. All are ingredients of an impatient system. At the same time, we have the structures which can provide care and social support to enrich the human spirit.

My goal in this chapter is to suggest the association of these problems and potentials and to encourage better planning to diminish the problems to every possible extent. We must understand revolution by resolution as a process. Metropolitan areas of the United States are negotiating systems. Further, cities are not masters of their fate. They are affected in many ways by events and forces national, state, and international over which they have no control.

A brief examination of the church role in the evolution of the American city illustrates this point. Digby Baltzell, in *The Protestant Establishment*, documents the political and economic power of the dominant Protestant systems particularly in the Northeastern cities, the older large cities in the nation. The earliest arrivals, in effect, got the jump on those who were to come. The large waves of immigrants who came to these new urban centers in the nineteenth and early twentieth centuries found a decision-power system in place. It was different from anything in Europe however. These cities were not based on a burgher model. The huge waves of immigrants who became the major population bases of the great urban centers were poor, Catholic, and Jewish. In order to gain entry into the political and economic mainstream, the religious and employee groups mobilized their institutional systems. They organized politically; they built hospitals and schools; they organized unions. The entire approach, as a strategy, was to seize control or at least gain entry for their people.

The institutional forms had then two open purposes: (1) resolution of specific needs for people not served by the system in place and (2) a subtle but direct advocacy for inclusion into the decision-making structure of the cities. This process and dynamic tension shaped the American city for at least a century. In effect, the great urban centers of America were spaces where people "became" Americans for, in fact, there were precious few natives there. The cities were almost alien outposts to the rural populations who were essentially Protestant. Michael Novak in *The Unmeltable Ethnics* observes that the dominant position of attitudes toward cities as "foreboding, evil, dangerous" places emerged during this period of Catholic-Jewish-Protestant estrangement.

To understand Boston, Pittsburgh, Chicago, Philadelphia, Baltimore, or New York, one must comprehend the historical importance of religious forms. The Irish in Boston were mobilized, organized through the special form of the Catholic Church. The institutions of the Church created a parallel resolution system which gradually took power. To suggest that any leader of New York can emerge without the support of the Jewish constituency is naive. These religious institutions pulled together fragmented nationality and language groups into a new uniquely American phenomenon. What the cardinal is saying might be front-page news in Chicago. And, it is no accident that Saint Patrick's Cathedral is physically in direct juxtaposition to the economic centers of New York. Inclusion for representation and participation has a long tradition in these centers through the mechanisms and programs of the Church.

The Southern and Western cities came later in the historical evolution of American cities. Their populations emerged from two new sources of people: second generation urbanites relocating for new opportunities and a new rural-to-urban movement. The Protestants and newer Americans began to build new kinds of places: Atlanta, Dallas, Los Angeles, Phoenix, and Houston. The role of the great church institutions was a bit different. The Protestant tradition was protective. It organized and had a response to institution building in order to protect its membership from this curious space called urban. The goal of many Baptist institutions was to deny the nature of cities, to create an alternative to the inclusion dynamic. Hospitals, schools, social service programs, and recreational activities were organized to provide safe havens in this "dangerous" environment. Political commentary, sharing of government resources, even sharing between denominations of the Protestant groups was not part of this tradition. These cities become confusing to the Yankee arrival in much the same manner that Southerners have been confused about the Northern centers. Those who are confused as to why the later groups of blacks who come to the Northern centers are different in their challenge have not examined the issue that they are Protestant and Southern in background.

Assumptions

Because of rapid change and the lag in institutional responses, our American cities can be described simultaneously as efficient and chaotic. We are a responding system. Our cities universally have major crises in housing, crime, traffic congestion, air, water, and noise pollution, poverty, unemployment, loneliness, and social agency organization. Traffic in Los Angeles is a result of an auto-based city development which has produced a sprawl of structures and resources with a fairly low density of population. New York was earlier in development but abstractly shares a congestion problem in its antiquated subway system. There are real differences in particulars but not in substance; in both cities, mobility can be a real problem.

The principal issue in all of the problems facing American cities today is in the context of scale. To suggest that we have little experience with mammoth populations should come as no surprise. To reemphasize that resolutions for yesterday do not necessarily provide insight for today is not terribly helpful. Scale produces problems. It makes it difficult to produce networks of people for problem solving. It encourages enclave strategies, such as neighborhood organizations and full-time professional agencies. *Probably the greatest problem facing us in today's American city is the separation of the people into these enclaves of area or occupation without relating them to the whole.*

Racism in housing and employment is a pervasive aspect of our American cities. The issue of scale and resulting social isolation creates a dilemma to be resolved. The question of where to organize the negotiating table becomes critical. The courts and federal government can order desegregation. The extent to which desegregation accomplishes the goal of an equitable educational environment depends entirely on the ability of the urban populations to participate in the decision. It is not unrealistic to suggest that success in the evolution to a "new society" is rare.

In spite of these scale problems, or possibly as a result of them, certain great neutral turfs have emerged institutionally. American cities have most of the world's great symphonies, opera companies, theater groups, and museums. In communications, no single society in history has the variety of stimuli from radio and television that we have in these cities. We are informed at a pace which staggers the imagination.

Every city in the United States lays claim to several universities, public and private, in its midst or locale. The study of our society has become a major department in each and every one of these campuses. A part of the rich tradition of our cities is reflected in the diversity and excitement of the college in the American city. NYU, Columbia, UCLA, University of Chicago, University of Pittsburgh, Boston University, Georgia Tech., University of Houston, USC, Marquette—each of these major urban university's student bodies, curricula, and activities reflect and enrich their respective cities. Scale makes it possible for these centers of activity to have unique roles in a society of new communication demands.

Establishment, Change, and Scale: the American City Today

Since 1910 no great, new city spaces have emerged. Phenomena such as the spread of population into suburban centers, satellite cities, back and forth to small city centers are a constant process. In the early part of this century, the South was a population base for new immigrants to the Northern cities. Blacks from the Southern region poured into Chicago, New York, Detroit, Cleveland, Philadelphia. Southern whites moved from Appalachia to Cincinnati, Dayton, Louisville, and Chicago. The draw for these populations was employment. Our Northern cities were becoming great world industrial centers, demanding large numbers of entry level employees.

World War II was a turning point for population movements. The mobilization of our young people to serve in the armed forces created a mobility pressure unheard of in world history. In a decade after that war, the population equivalent of Scandinavia moved West. It is hard today to realize that California had only six million people in 1940. Today its population is larger than that of Canada. A single continuous city 450 miles by 10 to 20 miles exists all the way from San Diego to San Francisco. Phoenix, which is approaching a total population of one million, had 65,000 people at the end of the war. Dallas and Houston were less than one-third their present size.

Central city USA was still the strongest population center of urban spaces in 1950. These central cities had a full spectrum of social classes with attendant social services and institutions. Such can certainly not be said for today. Central cities of America are increasingly places for rich and poor, young and old, with the middle groups increasingly in the outer suburban zones. The center cities have other highly specialized kinds of people. We could understand Greenwich Village in 1945 as an aberration characteristic of New York City. This great city was, after all, not at all truly representative of America. To realize that we now must respond politically to the gay vote in Atlanta, Dallas, Houston, Seattle, and elsewhere should illustrate quickly the point of the changes upon us. Certain central cities now are almost entirely adult havens. San Francisco is a city almost without children.

Those who talk about preserving and enhancing the American family as a traditional model of an extended family form—parents, children, grandparents—are obviously talking about an America which in our central cities does not exist. We have moved in one generation from a social system organized for ethnics to a large-scale system of single purpose groups in our central cities. In the East and North, this has occurred through out-migration and replacement; in the South and West, through growth and in-migration. The reality facing service agencies in central cities are large populations with particular needs: apartments for singles (Dallas has one apartment complex for 19 thousand singles as an example); entertainment zones for young adults; districts where there are high numbers of runaways. We face cities where large numbers of people are unserved by anyone or anything in a spectrum of huge demand. The fact is we don't even know where large numbers are located or even that they exist. After the riots in Detroit, Ford offered jobs on a first-come-first-hired basis to four thousand people. Forty thousand lined up for this opportunity. Henry Ford II commented that the shock was not just the number; it was that according to traditional records—such as birth certificates, voting registration, or permanent addresses—many of these people "did not exist."

Every political and social institution in American cities is struggling with this volatile system. Addison, Texas, had 800 persons in 1968; 7,000 in 1980, of whom 98 percent were in apartments. With over 5,000 voters, the highest turnout has been less than 400 for a liquor vote. This suburb of Dallas does not have one public school, has only one church of twenty members, no member of city council to even serve a full term, no volunteers in any social agencies, and only 12 percent native Texans.

In the move to suburbia of the middle groups, in terms of both age and social class, other kinds of problems have developed. The number of working mothers has produced a phenomenon of middle-class, "latch-key" children. In Arlington, Texas, a middle-class suburb of Dallas and Fort Worth, with 160,000 population, there are 11,000 children under age ten with no adult in the home for a minimum of eight hours a day.

What does all this mean for institutions such as the church? It means we now see specialized ministries and new skill demands. We see churches exploring and expanding services to singles, to young adults, organizing day-care programs; dealing with family crises in a plethora of manners; handling problems, such as divorce and illegitimacy; and trying to assist congregations to deal with new and different racial- and interest-group populations.

To suggest that American cities are happy places is to play a statistical game. A better assessment is to describe these spaces as places where people have to make new and different kinds of decisions for which we as institutional representatives are not always ready to assist. Few church leaders are ready to come out front to acknowledge our vulnerability to drugs, alcohol, to individual despair, to the issue of teenage sexuality and the resulting number of illegitimate births. A strong ethos in the church movement is to provide a meaningful alternative for the society— the haven. To suggest, however, that this constitutes real success is quite debatable.

The Challenge

The American city is in trouble; and when the city is in trouble, the country is in trouble. The symptoms are these: our cities are losing population, jobs, fiscal solvency, a sense of neighborhood and community, and the convenience, safety, and attractiveness that were the central cities' main reasons for being. Our cities are short on justice, tranquillity, and general welfare. Our institutions were prepared for a different city and are unresponsive and/or overwhelmed.

Jobs change in our economy. Jobs are leaving our central cities. So are people, both to suburbs and to the newer regions of the country. As the affluent middle class and skilled blue-collar workers have moved, the population left behind in the cities is increasingly a dependent one with little ability to finance the cities' service needs. This has exacerbated the movement, causing even larger numbers to leave. Institutions, such as human service agencies, education, and the church, are in a stressful period.

The debate on how to resolve these new challenges takes several forms. First, we see a strong traditional polarization strategy—far left or far right, both of which essentially reject the present as unsavable. Second, we see a resurgence of new strategies—those who are willing to minister in new ways. This latter group says the past has insights but no answers. I see in the latter group a vision of hope. So for the church, the challenges are clear in this series of questions:

1. Should the institutional church concentrate on its traditional support base? If so, it will find itself relegated to smaller proportions of the population and an alien to the city.
2. Should the church maintain its present traditional congregational form? Is this appropriate in a rapidly changing, highly mobile society of young persons, for example?
3. What are the needs the church should address? Obviously, the size-scale dimensions of certain problems are beyond the scope of any traditional system of church services. The strong demand for sensitive balance of a voice for the respect of the human as an individual and group member is called for.
4. Does all this mean that what the church is presently doing is wrong? Absolutely not is the only answer appropriate. What it means is that we must return to the old neighborhoods with some new approaches. A nation can manage and protect its citizens, but it cannot heal their social and personal wounds in the spirit of unity. The mechanisms of the church in our age are called to enhance "community" through fellowship.

The challenge of this thing called the American city is unique. It is unique because the nature and history of this phenomena says, It can be done. Those who argue that the age of institution building is over are only acknowledging the demand to start again.

There are despair agents who say the city is the home of the devil. I argue that this is true to the extent we permit it to be. There are those who say we cannot afford to do what is needed. Any model that will work must involve the participants. Have we so quickly forgotten how poor Baptist and many other Protestant congregations were, typically, but forty to fifty years ago? Yes, it will take money but, most important, it will take *ideas, commitment,* and *flexibility.* The American city is our future.

3

Our Mandate for Reaching Urban America
William M. Pinson, Jr.

One day recently I left the campus of Golden Gate Baptist Theological Seminary, where I work, and drove to downtown San Francisco for a meeting. Following the route which I had often taken—across the Golden Gate Bridge, through the edge of the Presidio, up Lombard and Van Ness to California, up and down California Street behind a cable car, through Chinatown—I arrived at my destination. On that day, I seemed more than usually aware of the people and the setting. Approximately five million persons live in the San Francisco Bay urban area—persons from scores of ethnic and language groups, of all ages and economic conditions, with a bewildering variety of life-styles. Standing on California Street in the canyon created by the skyscrapers, I asked myself, *What am I, the product of a small town in the Bible Belt, doing in this huge, secular metropolis?*

In many ways, I was a stranger in a foreign land. Having grown up in a small town where everyone in our school was the same color and spoke with the same accent, the clatter, complexity, and challenge of the urban area seemed strange to me even after several years of living in it. Knowing everyone I met on the streets, having Christian standards upheld in the school and community, seeing almost all my friends and neighbors going to church—these were the kinds of factors which shaped my early life. None of these prevail in the urban area where I now live.

Why, indeed, should I be here? The tug of my upbringing is to flee the noise and din of the city to the peace and quiet of the small town. Furthermore, doomsday prophets warn us to flee from the cities—for they will soon collapse in economic catastrophe. Indeed, more and more people seem to be moving from urban to

suburban areas and even to small towns and the open country.
*Why am I in one of America's vast urban centers? Should I
take my family and whisk them away to some safer, quieter place?*
As I reflected on these questions, I realized the answer was really
quite simple. I had followed the call of God to minister and to serve
in an urban setting. My study of the Bible and the human
condition had led me to an ever increasing conviction that the
urban area is where the work of God in our day must be
concentrated. I'm aware that many modern-day Jonahs, called to
minister in contemporary Ninevehs, are going in the opposite
direction. Frankly, there are times in which many are tempted to
follow them. But if we're true to the high calling of God in Christ
Jesus, we must stay where he has placed us.

In a sense, my own personal experience parallels that of most
Southern Baptists. Once a denomination of churches in the open
country and small towns, we have become increasingly a
denomination of urban areas. Many are still not comfortable there.
Our roots are in rural America. The tug to the safety of the towns
and suburbs is strong. Yet if we are true to the mandate of God, we
must stay in the cities. And God's mandate clearly points us to
reach urban America. At least four factors make up that mandate:
the biblical revelation, the human condition, divine compassion,
and Christian mission.

Biblical Revelation

The only solid foundation for a mission to urban America is
biblical truth. As the inspired Word of God, the Bible is true; we
ought to believe its teachings. The Bible is absolutely trustworthy;
we ought to follow its instructions. The Bible is our authority for
faith and practice; we ought to obey its commands. If the Bible
does not deal with a mandate to reach the cities, then we need not
try. But if the Bible mandates such a mission, we ought to be
involved in an all-out effort to reach the cities for Christ.

The biblical revelation begins in a garden, the Garden of
Eden. However, it moves toward a city as a symbol of hope, the city
of God, the new Jerusalem. The Bible says, "I saw a new heaven
and a new earth: for the first heaven and the first earth were passed

away; and there was no more sea. And I, John, saw the holy city, the new Jerusalem, coming down from God out of heaven, prepared as a bride adorned for her husband" (Rev. 21:1-2). The last chapter of the Bible declares, "Blessed are they that do his commandments, that they may have right to the tree of life, and may enter in through the gates into the city" (Rev. 22:14). God is pushing the history of the world toward that city which is to come (see Heb. 13:14). If we're tempted to think of the city as something representative of evil, we need to remember that God also uses the city as a symbol of hope.

Throughout the biblical revelation, cities figure prominently in the record. When the children of Israel came from the desert to take the Promised Land, the ancient city of Jericho was the first obstacle encountered. The Hebrews, having lived in the desert for years, were intimidated by the cities, but the walls of the city fell before the power of God. The event at Jericho demonstrates that a city, no matter how pagan, can be captured for God by people dedicated to him and to his purposes, willing to follow his commands. Often the cities intimidate us as Christians with deep rural roots. We're tempted to slink back into the desert. But Jericho encourages us to march forward, to take the cities for Christ.

Other cities play a large role in the Old Testament record. God sent Jonah to preach to the people of Nineveh. At first Jonah refused, but ultimately he repented and proclaimed God's message to the people of Nineveh. Nineveh was a pagan city, yet the people repented and a great revival erupted. Clearly even the pagan cities of our world may be receptive to the Word of God.

In the Old Testament, Babylon became the symbol of oppression and evil, a reputation it carried into the New Testament. Babylon reminds us that cities are often centers of evil, corrupt, and unjust persons; we cannot take sin lightly.

Much of the biblical revelation centers in the city of Jerusalem. God clearly cared for Jerusalem and sent his prophets to declare to the inhabitants the way of life and peace. Frequently the people ignored the prophets' word from God and disaster came. God continues to love the cities of the world and to send his spokesmen to declare the way to life. Unfortunately, cities continue to rebel against his word and the result is destruction, disaster, and death.

God chose Jerusalem as the site for the ultimate revelation of himself in human history through Jesus the Christ. Jesus, the Word of God incarnate, was born in Bethlehem which is just a short walk from Jerusalem. Immediately outside the city walls, Jesus was crucified, dying for the sins of the world. From a tomb somewhere near Jerusalem, Jesus emerged alive, the resurrection becoming a historical fact. Thus the three most significant events in history—the incarnation, the crucifixion, and the resurrection of Christ—took place at a city, the city of Jerusalem.

The New Testament shows that cities figured prominently in the spread of the good news about Jesus Christ. Mission strategy in the New Testament era concentrated on the cities. Therefore, a number of the books in the New Testament carry the names of ancient cities where churches were established—Rome, Ephesus, Corinth, Thessalonica, Colossae.

With such an emphasis in the Bible on cities, it is not surprising that persons who have saturated their lives with Scripture have been especially concerned about the cities. The people of God who have felt the heartbeat of the Scriptures understand that God's major battles are fought in the cities. Great pastors, such as Charles Haddon Spurgeon and George W. Truett, have spent their ministries in great cities. William Booth launched the Salvation Army in response to the vast needs of the cities of his day. Evangelists, such as Dwight L. Moody, Billy Sunday, and Billy Graham, have concentrated their soul-winning efforts in cities. Faced with today's increasing urbanization, we can do no less.

The Bible emphasizes three matters which give us a mandate to reach cities—the human condition, the divine compassion, and the Christian mission. Indeed, these call for us to reach people everywhere, in rural areas as well as urban, but they spotlight the urgency of reaching the multitudes compressed into the cities.

The Human Condition

The Bible reveals to be true what we conclude from experience and observation: all people everywhere are sinful and lost.

The Bible says, "For all have sinned and come short of the glory of God" (Rom. 3:23). The Genesis 3 account of Adam's and Eve's disobedience of God shows that sin affected their relationship with God and ours also. Eternal death is the heritage of all: by human nature we are sinners; by choice we are sinners (see Rom. 5:12-21).

The effect of humanity's turning away from God in sin is evident everywhere. One finds cruelty and injustice, thievery and lying, hatred and jealousy in all places—in country towns and metropolitan high rises. But in the cities, the effect of sin is compounded because of the vast number of persons crowded together, interacting with one another. Crime, violence, injustice, pollution—all of these are concentrated in the cities. Certainly they exist in rural America. But what is hardly noticeable scattered widely across a rural landscape becomes terrifyingly obvious when concentrated in cities.

Urban persons are no more lost in sin than rural persons are. But the effects of lostness seem magnified in the masses of urban America. Rape, robbery, drug abuse, alcoholism, murder, and oppression abound. Poverty and perversion, loneliness and hopelessness litter the metropolitan landscape.

The effect of sin is seen not only in individuals and their interpersonal relations but also in the institutions of society, which are more prominent in the cities than in rural America. Governmental, business, educational institutions—all developed to benefit human life—when corrupted by sin, twist and mangle human existence. Greed, selfishness, and lust for power pervert institutions. Thus the mandate to minister to urban America includes not only individuals but also institutions and social structures. Governments, businesses, schools, and families all need our attention.

Christians ought to have a realistic view of how difficult dealing with cities is because they realize urban problems have spiritual roots. Urban dwellers are sinners. Christians should know the hard reality of sin and expect no quick, easy solutions. The only hope for lost persons is Christ. What we do and what we say in the cities must center in Christ. Jesus Christ is unique. Each aspect of his uniqueness relates to his mission and to ours.

For example, only Jesus was the Word made flesh (see John

1:14). He is "the image of the invisible God" (Col. 1:15). "In him dwelleth all the fulness of the Godhead bodily" (Col. 2:9). The purpose of the incarnation was redemption: "God was in Christ, reconciling the world unto himself" (2 Cor. 5:19). The indicative of the incarnation is the imperative for missions; Jesus said, "As my Father hath sent me, even so send I you" (John 20:21).

Only Jesus was perfect, without sin, and died in order that sinners could be forgiven and saved from the consequences of their sin: "being now justified by his blood, we shall be saved from wrath through him" (Rom. 5:9). Self-acclaimed messiahs abound in the cities of America. They differ in their methods of saviorship but are all alike in one regard: none is perfect, all are flawed. Only Jesus is the sinless Savior.

Only Jesus rose from the dead, alive to live forever. Because of his resurrection, he lives in those who invite him into their lives, empowering them to carry out his commands, even in the difficult places of the cities. Paul, the effective missionary to cities, let us in on the secret to his effectiveness when he wrote, "I am crucified with Christ: nevertheless I live; yet not I, but Christ liveth in me" (Gal. 2:20), and "I can do all things through Christ which strengtheneth me" (Phil. 4:13).

Only Jesus is coming again in judgment and glory. The fact of his return adds a note of urgency to our mission in the cities. The numbers are so great and the needs are so huge that we do not have time to dally. Jesus did not tell us when his return would be. In fact, he said, "It is not for you to know the times or the seasons, which the Father hath put in his own power" (Acts 1:7). He did indicate that his return would be sudden and that we should be prepared. The best way to be prepared is to live godly lives and be busy sharing the word about Jesus with the lost world; he may come at any time and terminate our efforts.

Many saviors are being peddled in the cities of our land. New cults and sects spring into existence every year. Claims and counterclaims are made about this savior and that, this remedy and that. Many good things can be done for the urban dwellers of our land, but there is only one way that offers ultimate hope—the way to Christ.

Indeed, Jesus is unique. The Bible teaches that the only alternative to believing in Jesus Christ is to go to hell. Jesus said of himself, "I am the way, the truth, and the life: no man cometh unto the Father, but by me" (John 14:6). The Bible says of Jesus, "Neither is there salvation in any other: for there is none other name under heaven given among men, whereby we must be saved" (Acts 4:12). Jesus is not the best among many saviors but the only Savior; that truth forms a large part of our mandate for reaching the cities.

In the cities, all people need to hear the word of salvation about Christ, for all are lost without him. For some urban dwellers, our only ministry may be to share the eternal hope in Jesus Christ. For them there are no temporal solutions to their problems; social change will not come soon enough to alter the suffering of millions now alive. Without lessening the need for Christian social action or reducing the gospel to promises of pie in the sky by-and-by, we must not be ashamed to tell the suffering masses of our cities about a city where God will wipe away all tears from their eyes and there will be no more grief, crying, or pain.

Divine Compassion

God clearly cares about the plight of the cities and of the persons in them. The fact that he sent his Son to be their Savior is the best indication of divine compassion. And Jesus, in the incarnation, demonstrated divine love for urban humanity. Perhaps the most poignant picture in the Bible of God's compassion for the city is Jesus weeping over Jerusalem.

God loves all persons, not just a select few. The Bible teaches that he loves us in spite of our sin. He loves all races, classes, nationalities, and personality types. As the incarnate Son of God, Jesus made clear that God loves all persons and does not want any to perish. Jesus' mission included Jew and Gentile, male and female, slave and free, poor and rich, weak and strong, sick and well, dull and bright, profane and religious, young and old. To read the record of Jesus' ministry is to be staggered by the variety of people for whom he demonstrated love. Clearly all people in the cities are the object of his love.

Jesus again and again expressed concern for all nations. He told the disciples, "Go ye therefore, and teach all nations, baptizing them in the name of the Father, and of the Son, and of the Holy Ghost: Teaching them to observe all things whatsoever I have commanded you; and lo, I am with you alway, even unto the end of the world" (Matt. 28:19-20). In the cities of America, God has brought the nations of the world together. We can carry out part of God's mandate to reach all nations by reaching the cities of America.

The Bible reveals God as having a special compassion for the poor, weak, oppressed, and unlovely. Jesus spent much of his ministry caring for persons whom others had either ignored or rejected. William G. Tanner, president of the Home Mission Board of the Southern Baptist Convention, writes:

> Our mission to America is not urgently spelled out for us in terms of money, programs, under-evangelized cities, or unchurched communities, but in terms of people—people that Christ loved and loves— people for whom he died. No, urgency is not found in graphs, infrastructured strength, progress charts, and success symbols. Urgency is written in the blue-black bruises on the body of a battered child in Phoenix. Urgency is fleshed out in the painted face of a teenage prostitute cruising on Tenth and Peachtree. Urgency is distilled in the killing loneliness of an aged couple in Miami waiting for letters that never come and the phone calls that are never placed. Urgency is vocalized in the withdrawal screams of an addict in Chicago without enough bread for his next fix. Urgency is incarnate in a young woman in Oakland whose search for a job ended in frustration and who now stands over the body of a convenience store operator with a smoking handgun. Urgency is etched in the face of a young mother in Dallas—no lights, no water, no heat, and her man long gone. See them? Hear them? Feel them?[1]

The Bible reveals that the compassion of God is not only for all kinds of persons but also for all aspects of a person. God is concerned about people's souls, but he is also concerned about their bodies, emotions, and minds. Jesus loved all of a person and demonstrated that by his ministry. He fed the hungry, healed the sick, cured the emotionally disabled, fed truth to the open-minded, and told about eternal life which was available from the Father through the Son. As recorded in Matthew 25, Jesus taught that we are to care for the total needs of others—providing food, clothing, water, and compassion to those who lack them.

Human need is concentrated in the cities. Human need appears more acute in urban than in nonurban places. People are poor in rural areas as well as in urban, but in many ways urban poverty has a deeper agony. In the country the poor might at least have a chance to plant a garden, catch a fish, pick up free firewood, and breathe clean air. In the cities, food is obtainable only from grocery stores or garbage cans. Heat must be purchased with money, which is often scarce. Air is fouled not only by the normal pollutants of a city but also by those special afflictions of the poor— inadequately ventilated rooms, open-flame heat, urine-drenched hallways, rotting garbage, and accumulated layers of filth.

Because God has compassion for all persons and all of a person, so must we. The message of the Scriptures is that we are to pattern our lives after the character of God. Jesus said, "Be ye therefore perfect, even as your Father which is in heaven is perfect" (Matt. 5:48). In other words, be like God. As the incarnate Son of God, one of Jesus' basic commands was, "Follow me!" To follow him is to have the compassion he had.

Jesus also indicated that we are to love God with all of our beings and to love our neighbors as we love ourselves—and he defined neighbor as anyone in need (see Matt. 22:34-40). If we love people, how can we refuse to provide food for the hungry, clothes for the naked, pure water for the thirsty, comfort for the suffering, and the gospel for the lost who walk in darkness? Cities are concentrations of human need clamoring for our concern, action, and ministry. God loves the cities—the persons who make them up, all of them, and the needs of each person, all of them. We are to love like that. Those facts make up a big part of our mandate for reaching the cities.

Today's Christians should be right at home caring for total human need in the cities. Long before government agencies and private organizations became interested in welfare or social reform, church people were active in these areas. Education, medical care, relief for the poor, and similar programs for centuries were almost solely the concern of churches. Before poverty programs were part of the government activities, Christians were struggling to ease the plight of the poor in the slums and inner-city ghettos. Great churches have never been confined to honeycombs of classrooms for education and barns for preaching but have been involved in ministry to total human need in the way of Christ.

The Christian Mission

The Bible indicates that the nature of our salvation in Christ calls for us to share the good news about him with others. We are saved to serve. We have been set free from the penalty and power of sin in order to help free others. We do this by telling others about Christ and ministering to them in his name.

Witness and ministry, according to the Bible, are not just to be shared with those immediately around us but with persons throughout the world. In fact, a frequent command in the Bible is to go and tell. Certainly we should go to where the masses of people are gathered—in the cities.

Our mission is to take the gospel to everyone everywhere. If you are on mission, you have been sent to carry out a task away from your normal home base and you have accepted the assignment. Mission implies inconvenience, risk, sacrifice, and even danger. Why would someone get involved in such? The Bible indicates many reasons. One is because God tells us to. Another is because we should love and care for other persons. And another is our own welfare, for there is no complete job in the Christian life apart from being on mission to share the good news. Jesus' promise to be with us always is linked to his command to go to all people everywhere (see Matt. 28:20). Those busy about the mission of Jesus know of the empowering presence of the living Christ. Perhaps the reason many seem to be so little aware of the Lord's presence is that they are not on mission with and for him.

And how are we to go about our mission? The Bible supplies several guidelines. For example, the earliest Christians on mission majored on the cities. So should we. The New Testament pattern was for Christians to go from city to city sharing. Paul, the missionary to the Gentiles, clearly demonstrated this strategy in his ministry. Apparently he spent little time in the rural areas or small towns. He went to the cities. He spent time in cities such as Corinth, Ephesus, and Athens. In a sense Paul was following the example of Jesus who preached not only in rural Galilee but also in metropolitan Jerusalem.

A feature of mission in the city is the involvement of all believers in sharing the gospel. The task cannot be one by pastors alone. The numbers of persons who need help is too large for a few professional religionists to handle. In rural churches, perhaps people can be allowed the luxury of spectator religion with the preacher being the performer and the congregation being the spectators. But that won't work in the city. There is absolutely no way for the multitudes to be reached by hired professionals alone. The only way the masses can be touched is by all of the people of God being on mission for Christ. The apostle Paul realized this. He spent much of his time equipping new converts to share and minister to others.

Churches must play a key role in the mission of reaching cities. In the New Testament, churches were not identified with buildings but with people. Churches were congregations of believers; they were the people of God called into a fellowship to function as the body of Christ in the world. They had structure and organization which enabled them to function effectively, but structure was not the reason for their effectiveness. They were effective because the people who made them up had deep faith, a strong prayer life, a courage to witness, and a willingness to minister. They did not fire media missiles to reach the masses but rather engaged in hand-to-hand combat by relating personally to those who populated the cities. Churches are still God's method of reaching the cities. And churches today must reach the cities in the way the New Testament churches did: by personal relationship with those who need the gospel and need ministry.

Local churches must be structured to deal with the situations in which they exist. Standardized, predeveloped plans imposed on a local congregation will not meet the needs of the complex, modern city. Variety and flexibility are demanded. Churches in the city come in many shapes, sizes, and locations. A city is in a constant state of flux. There is no orthodoxy of program or structure. What works for one church may not work for another. God opens new doors every morning, and we must have the courage to walk through them. We should experiment with new approaches and methods. This does not mean abandoning old methods simply because they are old. The test is not, Is it old or new? but Does it serve to effectively carry out the mission of the church? Many traditional ways work well today; but in Christ, we have been set free to try the different.

Baptists, for example, traditionally have been nontraditional. We have been willing to open new streets in the city of God. We were lumped with the radical wing of the Reformation for good reason. We were regarded with suspicion by the monarchies of Europe because we favored new forms of government. The established churches of America showed us ill will because we proposed new church structures. Baptists spread across the frontier like a prairie fire because we abandoned traditional methods of establishing churches and training ministers. Other Baptist groups regarded Southern Baptists as radical and unorthodox when we adopted a board and convention approach to denominationalism. Today, if we are to be a part of reaching the cities, our Baptist genius for developing creative, innovative, and effective approaches to Christian ministry must be kept alive.

Churches must learn that they cannot handle the challenge of the city alone. Corporate action is often needed to deal with personal problems in the city. In rural areas, problems can usually be cared for on a personal basis. If a neighbor is sick, friends help harvest his crops. If his house burns, neighbors pitch in to build and furnish another. Such an approach to human need is seldom workable in the city. Social issues, as well as personal human need, call for corporate action. If urban problems are to be cared for, churches must learn to express Christian love through social action. Churches in cities can help form community action groups to deal with specific problems, such as housing, pollution, crime, alcohol, and poverty.

As churches realize the need for social action as well as

personal ministry, they see that it is not enough to tutor the slow learner without also doing something about the social circumstances which caused him to be mentally deficient. They understand that it is not enough to provide clothes and food to the poor and do nothing about the near starvation wages many are paid. They form action groups to tackle the social problems of the city.

The Bible indicates that an effective mission to the city requires faithfulness in the face of difficulty. Reaching cities for Christ is difficult work. Urban dwellers are often hostile to those bearing the message of God. The Old Testament records prophet after prophet who was killed in Jerusalem. Jesus was crucified by city dwellers. Paul was executed in a city. Furthermore cities are often crowded, dangerous, noisy, and irritating. Their immensity threatens to overwhelm us—the task appears too large to accomplish. But simply because we cannot reach all cities or all of a particular city does not mean that we should not reach any cities or any part of a city. Paul was never successful in reaching all of the people in a city for Christ. But this did not keep him from reaching a great many. If we wait until we can accomplish everything, we will never accomplish anything.

Carrying out the mandate to reach the cities is often frustrating because of the constant change in urban areas. One can work for years establishing and growing a church in a city only to have much of that work seemingly wiped out by a shift in population caused by zoning changes or building a freeway. That is discouraging, but it should not paralyze our efforts. It is the doing of the task that is important and not the enduring of it. None of the churches established by Paul in the cities of his day have continued to exist. Many of the great urban congregations of yesterday have passed out of existence. But while they existed, these mission stations did vast good in the cities where they were located. Certainly we should strive to develop an enduring ministry, but we should not despair when changes in a city alter our ministry in a city.

Those who carry out God's mandate to reach the cities must endure pain, frustration, disappointment, and physical discomfort. Doing the will of God is seldom easy; worthwhile endeavors hardly ever are. God calls us to mission involvement which is almost always difficult. Going on mission for Christ means going to war with Satan and his legions, and war is costly. Go on mission in God's will and you may encounter conflict, resistance, persecution, and perhaps even death. Such difficulties do not mean you were outside the will of God. Being in the will of God usually involves constructive suffering. Paul knew suffering; he spoke about the fellowship of Christ's suffering (see Phil. 3:10). Suffering and following Christ naturally go together. After all, Jesus said, "If any man will come after me, let him deny himself, and take up his cross, and follow me" (Matt. 16:24). The Bible makes clear that Christians on mission for Christ in the city ought not be surprised by difficulty; they should expect it.

If the task of reaching the cities is so difficult, how can anyone carry it out? Surely on our own we will fail. But God has promised his power to those who go in his name. Jesus indicated that those who were faithful to be on mission for him would be indwelled with the power of the Holy Spirit. Up against impossible demands, we must seek power through prayer and fling wide our faith to catch the mighty rush of God's Spirit. Jesus promised that the Holy Spirit would lead us to all truth; faced with more needs than can possibly be met in the cities, we must follow the Spirit's leading to know what tasks to tackle. As the early missionaries reached out for the cities, they were both guided and empowered by the Holy Spirit. They were aware of the presence of the living Christ, as he had promised.

If carrying out the mandate to reach urban America is so difficult, why should we undertake it? There are many reasons. Because God says so; the One who gave us life has instructed us how to use that life—how can we ignore him? Because Jesus asked us to; the One who suffered and died that we might have eternal life tells us to go on mission to people everywhere—how can we say no? Because the Holy Spirit guides us to mission; the One who enables and empowers us if we are obedient bids us to try—how can we refuse? Because millions in the cities are lost without Christ; they will not know the way to life unless we tell them—how can we stay safely, securely within the familiar all of our lives in the face of such need? Because God rewards those who serve him in difficult places; the time of hardship on mission in urban America is but an instant in our eternity with God, who rewards his faithful servants in glorious ways—why should anyone trade the rewards of heaven for the comforts of the world? Because joy comes to those on mission in the cities where humanity is concentrated and human needs are magnified; we know joy when we are faithful to God's calling and purpose, joy in the midst of conflicts and difficulty—why would anyone shut the door to joy?

Conclusion

Some are called by God to serve in rural areas and in small towns and in the suburbs. People there need Christ also. But clearly many more are needed in the cities because that is where most people live and where people's needs are concentrated. The Bible being our authority, we have no option but to be on mission for Christ in the cities of America. Our mandate is to reach the cities. That calls for thousands of persons to be on mission for Christ in the cities. That means the establishment of hundreds of new loving, witnessing, ministering churches.

Our mandate for reaching urban America is clear. What if we fail to act? What if we go on with business as usual? What if we bog down in doctrinal or institutional feuds and ignore the plight of the cities? Perhaps God will raise up another people to do what we would not do. Or he may let the inevitable wages of our sin be paid—death: death in our cities as pollution, prejudice, and riot take their toll. Death of little children through hunger, rat bites, drugs, and violence. Death of our churches as they perish from neglect, racism, inflexibility, and the shame of failure to meet the challenges around them. Death of our freedom and democracy as revolutionaries capitalize on the intolerable situation created by our apathy to bring the cities crashing down around us. Death eternal to the multitudes in the cities who never clearly hear or see our witness unto Jesus Christ.

But if we respond with swift, courageous, massive action, we could write new chapters in the story of God's people. As our forefathers swept across the frontiers for Christ, let us take the cities for him too. In so doing, we will not only carry out God's mandate but we will also discover joy in being faithful to the heavenly vision, the new Jerusalem, the city of God.

Note

1. William G. Tanner, *Hurry Before Sundown* (Nashville: Broadman Press, 1981), p. 21.

4
The Cultural Captivity of Urban Churches
Larry L. McSwain

The contemporary community of Christian believers lives with the same tension of its first-century counterpart. The early church struggled constantly with the pressure of living in two worlds simultaneously. So the Bible is filled with multiple accounts of the pilgrimage of Jesus' disciples to live in the world while bringing to it the values of the kingdom of God. Jesus' high priestly prayer for his followers captured the dialectic that is inherent in Christian discipleship:

> "I do not pray that thou shouldst take them out of the world, but that thou shouldst keep them from the evil one. They are not of the world, even as I am not of the world. As thou didst send me into the world, so I have sent them into the world" (John 17:15-16, 18, RSV).

"In the world, but not of the world" seems to be the motto of this Johannine perception of our Lord's ministry and commission to his disciples. The apostle Paul used different language but communicated the same idea in his training of new converts within a variety of cultural contexts. The vehicles of Greek polytheism and philosophical thought were used by Paul to communicate Christian truth to the wise of Athens (Acts 17:22-34). Yet he warned his Roman readers to avoid conformity to the world in favor of the transforming power of committed service (Rom. 12:1-2). To his Corinthian friends, he confessed the treasure of the light of Christ shines through "earthen vessels" so the church may not claim glory that belongs to God (2 Cor. 4:7).

"Treasure in earthen vessels" aptly describes the dualism of the Christian church throughout its history. Which side of this dualism one chooses to emphasize determines the strategy of involvement in the world the church will have. H. Richard Niebuhr suggests five such choices have been made in Christian history to resolve the tension.[1] First, some have chosen the way of sectarian opposition to culture, emphasizing 1 John 2:15-17. This "Christ against culture" view stresses withdrawal by the church into a disciplined community, resisting its cultural setting. In this view, the function of the church is to build a wall between itself and the larger world.

Second, some in Christian history have emphasized the "Christ of culture," stressing accommodation between the two. Here the strategy is to find the best in culture which can be claimed for the church. Thus, the Christian community becomes a mirror of the best the culture has to offer.

Niebuhr said the third option was a synthesis of the two in an effort to develop a rational unit of faith and history. He called this view the "Christ above culture" approach in which the church as an institution becomes the mechanism for that unity. Thus, the church becomes the ladder by means of which Christ and culture are unified.

A fourth position is called "Christ and culture in paradox." Both live in tension with one another with each affecting separate realms. Christ judges the sin of every culture which can never be perfected this side of the eschaton. The church lives "between" the two in tension—between its loyalty to Christ and its identification with the world.

Niebuhr's final type is "Christ the transformer of culture" or the conversionist perspective. Culture is inherently evil, as in the dualism of the paradox type. But culture is God's creation, capable of redemption and becoming the matrix of God's action in human history. The church serves as a servant to become a participant in God's transforming kingdom as it comes to the world of imperfect persons and structures.

How can the church be this servant of transformation to the urban milieu of the present moment? First, by identifying its captivity to the culture as it stands against the meaning of God's kingdom and second by becoming captive to the kingdom which transforms all of life. In other words, the task of today's church is to get the world out of the churches and get the churches into the world.

Earthen Vessels: Captive to Cultural Forces

If the contemporary church is to fulfill its mission as a transformer of culture, it must understand the culture of which it is a part. The truth is always encapsulated in a human form.[2] That is the meaning of the incarnation. No church can exist apart from some culture. The question is not whether churches will reflect their culture but, rather, the kind of culture they reflect and whether it hinders their ability to bear witness to the truth of the gospel. Every church, thus, must decide to whom or what it will be captive. For the church, like individuals, finds its greatest freedom only when it has chosen the form of its slavery. Heinrich Schlier summarized his study of the New Testament understanding of freedom, "Man attains to self-control by letting himself be controlled."[3] Churches must choose the form of their cultural captivity. What then are the cultural forces with which churches must deal if they are to minister effectively to our urban context?

Captivity to ruralism. The first form of captivity most American Protestant church groups must face is their historical effectiveness in rural America. The theology of churches in the free church tradition was especially conducive to the planting of churches across the hinterland of America in its developing stages. The doctrine of the priesthood of the believer gave rise to the emergence of lay preachers who proclaimed the Word. They flowed westward in search of their "manifest destiny" along with other Americans. Where they went, churches were begun which grew with the towns and villages in which they were started. More hierarchical traditions, such as Roman Catholic and Episcopal churches, settled in the cities where there was sufficient population for a parish with available priestly leadership.

The consequence is that the styles of worship, forms of church organization, functions of clergy, symbols of faith, and avenues of building community within most Protestant groups, especially evangelical ones, are shaped by a rural heritage. For the 25 percent of the population which lives in nonmetropolitan America, this tradition is very much alive and well. But that tradition does not necessarily provide the theological and organizational resources needed for a metropolitan population which is three fourths of the people of the nation.

Should the rural traditions be abandoned? Of course not! They cannot be when in a denomination like the Southern Baptist Convention 62 percent of the churches and 48 percent of the church members are located in nonmetropolitan communities.[4] But neither will the power of Protestant faith be known in the city if mission strategy consists of transplanting rural faith forms in the city. How does a gospel of personal, individual accountability function in a setting in which evil structures destroy individual initiative and effort? Will the neighborliness of rural religion melt the anonymity of an urban high-rise apartment complex? Building-centered organizations and highly structured Sunday School programs may not fit a poor, ethnic neighborhood where the base for church is someone's living room. Expensive and highly professional media often are needed to communicate to urban persons indirectly and often impersonally. Rural expressions usually do not communicate in the urban context.

Captivity to numerical success. The most serious form of cultural captivity for today's churches is their commitment to nonbiblical definitions of numerical success. Surely there is an affirmation of evangelizing numbers of people in the New Testament. But equally valued is evangelism into a life-transforming gospel.

The churches of America are alive and vital in terms of any external measure of religious vitality. More people in America go to church more frequently for a greater variety of activities than any other nation of the world. A group of scholars analyzed recently the religious trends in America from 1950 to 1978 and found an amazing numerical strength, weekly participation, and positive feeling within American churches.[5] Churches are alive in the American context!

Now how could success be a form of captivity? In two ways. First, there is a captivity in terms of the cultural sources of this success. By and large, the numerical success is based upon a successful "churching" of respectable, upwardly mobile, employed persons who hold to traditional values. The "unchurched" tend to be those searching most desperately for an intellectually satisfying faith, those judged by the church for their moral failures, and those too poor or unrespectable to fit the expectations of churches for exemplary living.[6] The captivity of numerical success is to be found in that churches have evangelized those most easily evangelized. They are too often not willing to struggle with the unevangelized to communicate the love of Jesus Christ.

The second form of captivity consists of the powerlessness of popular religion in the American setting. The church has had its weakest impact historically when it was strongest. Popular religion loses its prophetic power and its mission consciousness. Popular religion is not synonymous with Christian faith. Rather, it is a "civilizing" of biblical faith into a civil religion which makes church involvement a form of social respectability. Whenever Christian faith becomes popular religion, it faces the dilemmas of the Danish church in Kierkegaard's time. It is the problem of becoming so sophisticated, so domesticated, so acceptable there is little power for change. The Word is heard so often everyone believes, no one behaves, and few listen. In his parable, "The Domestic Goose: A Moral Tale" the Danish prophet describes the church as a flock of geese:

> The sermon was essentially the same each time—it told of the glorious destiny of geese, of the noble end for which their master had created them—and every time his name was mentioned all of the geese curtsied and all of the ganders bowed their heads. They were to use their wings to fly away to the distant pastures to which they really belonged; for they were only pilgrims on this earth.[7]

None of the geese ever flew, however, for they were so overfed they could not fly. Some parallel could be drawn to the religious situation of the United States. The Gallup Polls of religion in this country consistently show high levels of belief in God (94 percent), high levels of membership in churches, fairly high levels of attendance (40 percent), and the relative importance of religion in personal life.[8] Yet 61 million adults remain unchurched, most church members know little of the content of the Bible, and behavior consistent with the norms of traditional biblical faith continues to be abandoned for secularism. Martin Marty charges:

> We have become a nation of metaphysical shoplifters, spiritual window-shoppers, pious cafeteria-liners. In the end our religious being everywhere tends to be nowhere. Ministers become chaplains to ethnic groups, or persons who keep the doors open to preside at weddings. But they have a hard time representing the legitimate and biblical kinds of power that go along with "organized," not diffused religion.[9]

Conservative evangelical Christians are especially vulnerable to this success syndrome. Using rather rigorous definitions of evangelical—a "born-again Christian" who believes the Bible literally and encourages others to accept Jesus Christ—the Gallup Poll estimates 20 percent of all adults are evangelical. Evangelicals are more likely to be members of a church, attend it regularly, and experience their religion as important than nonevangelicals.

Given such growing popularity, it will become increasingly more difficult for denominations and Christians so identified to avoid their responsibility of involvement in urban ministry. Yet, one half of all evangelicals live in the South and 45 percent are age fifty or older. Does this represent a form of cultural captivity to traditional communities of tradition-minded persons? Is such faith prepared to move to the marketplace environment of the world cities where it will be in a minority position? Can the imperative for witness so essential to missionary faith cross the geographic, social, ethnic, and educational barriers which presently surround the faith perspective of most evangelical congregations? It must if the faith of the contemporary churches is to have any transforming power.

Captivity to an aging structure. A third cultural force with which churches must deal is the "graying" of American society. In the past decade, there has been an amazing transformation in the dynamic of America from a growing, innovative, and dynamic society to one of stability, retrenchment, and pessimism. It is a mood which captures the political, economic, and religious arenas of the land. The median age of society has changed from twenty-six years of age in the mid-sixties to over thirty-one in 1980.

I have described the churches as alive and vital. But are they well? Some ominous signs are apparent, and they are larger than a cloud the size of a man's hand. While there is much strength within religious institutions, the trends are in the direction of decline. From 1957 to 1970, the proportion of Americans saying religion was losing influence grew from 13 to 75 percent. The number dropped back down to 45 percent in 1976 but has begun to move upward since then. Church attendance has receded from 49 percent in 1955 to 41 percent in 1978. The proportion of Americans receiving religious training as children declined from 94 percent in 1952 to 83 percent today.[10]

In themselves there is little alarm to be sounded by these data. Trends change. These declines are moderate. Revival could transform them into new directions overnight.

Except for one disturbing factor which accounts for most of the change, much of this statistical decline can be accounted for by the defection of one generation of people from the church. Most of the loss in membership and religious participation can be accounted for by persons who were born between the years 1940-1960. Ironically, the children of the churches are becoming the churches' biggest institutional problem.[11]

Remember, these are the folk who are young and median adults today. They were children in Sunday School in overwhelming numbers in the traditional 1950s. They have heard the biblical message in some form. As much as any other group in our society, they have heard the traditional message of the church. They went to school when the pledge of allegiance was said daily and prayer was offered in many classrooms. They were baptized young, went to church camp in the summer, and attended Sunday night church.

But they also went to college. They went in overwhelming numbers, glutting the higher education system at a moment of unprecedented social ferment. They encountered a rampant scientism stimulated by Sputnik and the race with the Soviets for supremacy in space. They were assaulted by a militant civil rights movement which forced the hard choices of jumping off the middle of the fence into advocacy or resistance. They encountered a new morality of sexual permissiveness promulgated by the purveyors of porn and popularized nontheologians. They were caught on the horns of the dilemma of patriotic duty to fight in Southeast Asia or resist the war.

A minority of older adults joined forces with them in that process. Those who did tended to be the more highly educated—their teachers and leaders. A strange coalition emerged in the form of a new elite of tough, educated, and battered young adults and older professionals. The seventies hit and what happened?

For a multitude, the battering was too much. The traditional religious and moral values of childhood were inadequate. So marriage began a slow process of dissolution. Divorce skyrocketed, and a tear in the fabric of marriage was observed. Work for achievement was replaced for a philosophy of work for meaning and possession.

This generation of young adults began to embrace a new pluralism religiously. Sect groups and cults of both Christian and non-Christian varieties attracted the most isolated of this group. Alternative Christian forms sprung up—house churches, renewal groups, and neo-Pentecostals. Others became denominational switchers or dropouts, adopting a religion of civic piety with sophistication and avant-garde adoption of cultural values as the key components. Those who stayed in the church became enamored with new self-help therapies and participated in much of the self-centeredness of the "me decade" of the 1970s. The consequence is an interesting gap in the institutional church today. One finds a lower rate of attendance, participation, and commitment to traditional values in churches today among those who are twenty to forty than was the case among this age group in previous generations.

But something else happened to their younger brothers and sisters. While fewer in number, a more conservative and traditional mind-set is found among them. They are as committed to the church and traditional values as were previous generations of teenagers. According to a survey of nearly 19,000 graduating seniors in 1978, 56.6 percent attend a church with some degree of frequency.[12] Sixty percent consider their religion important and most have a high appraisal of religious institutions.

What is the implication of this situation? We have a nontraditional, highly-educated, young- and middle-adult group tenuously connected to churches in which the leadership over age forty and the teenagers are more nearly alike in values. This group often feels outside the institution because of a different value orientation. If ways are not found to minister effectively to the "middlescence" of this group without intense conflict, there could be a fifteen-year leadership vacuum within denominational churches. On the other hand, if this young adult group can be attracted into church leadership, the 1980s offer the potential of the greatest development of resources for Christian ministry that churches have ever known.

This young adult group lives in the city. The attraction of urbanism for education, employment opportunity, entertainment, and career advancement draws the young to the city. Some are able to fulfill their dreams while others find themselves with dried-up visions shattered by unemployment, poverty, and subsistence living. It is a group which has experienced more and earlier than any previous generation, and it does not accept simple answers to complex problems. As a group, these young adults marry later, have fewer children at an older age, have more income, and are heavily in debt in comparison with their elders.

In the meantime, the leadership of churches is aging rapidly. Local churches cry out for replacements to fill the gaps of retiring Sunday School teachers and the losses of church budgets carried by the leadership over age forty. Nowhere is this more apparent than in the urban churches with the greatest needs for leadership— inner city, transitional, and declining suburban congregations. As the congregation grows older, less likely are its chances of attracting the defected young adults into its life.

Captive to congregational uniformity. A final form of cultural captivity with which churches must deal is their homogeneity. Most congregations of Christians are found along the lines of social compatibility. The predominant form of urban church is the neighborhood church. In the past, urban neighborhoods have formed along social class, racial, and ethnic uniformity. So the

urban church developed as a reflection of its neighborhood homogeneity.

But urban neighborhoods give way with increasing rapidity to
change. There is a new pluralism being created today by the
suburbanization of racial and ethnic groups and the "gentrification"
of the urban core. More typically, the neighborhood context of the
average urban congregation is one of diversity. Even when it is not,
its institutions, such as the neighborhood school, are. Busing,
desegregation programs, and innovations in public-school systems
have created a much more diverse environment for school-age
children. The consequence is a rapidly changing matrix within
which the urban congregation must do its ministry. If the racially
segregated, socially uniform, and ethnically homogeneous congregational strategies which worked in the past are fostered in this new
urban environment, churches will become agents of fragmentation
in their communities.

The city is a pluralistic environment. More than three fourths
of the minority groups of the United States live in metropolitan
areas. More than one half of the black population and one half of
the Spanish population live in central cities. With more than thirty-
eight million nonwhite in the United States, a major challenge for
evangelical witness exists. Southern Baptists, as one such group
successful in growing in the past, have only begun to reach such
groups. Southern Baptist churches can claim in their membership
only 1 of every 331 blacks in the United States and 1 of every 122 of
Spanish origin. Any meaningful commitment to urban ministry is a
commitment to even greater pluralism within the churches, for
such a failure becomes a denial of the universal power of the gospel
to reach across cultures. As Benjamin Reist has written:

> If we share the gospel; and if we understand it at depth as it has
> been transmitted to us; and if my birthright, but not yours, resides
> in the cultural matrix out of which it has come to each of us; and if,
> furthermore, neither you nor I are willing to see that it can be
> fathomed in terms of your cultural history as well as mine—then the
> mere proclamation of the gospel by either of us denies the integrity,
> the reality, the potential of you, and in this sense feeds your long
> dying, a dying I have effected.[13]

The task of the gospel is not to call persons to a white Anglo-Saxon Protestantism. It is not to call persons to a black cultural experience, nor to a Mexican or Brazilian cultural experience. The gospel of Jesus Christ is transcultural. It calls all persons out of their culture in the transforming power of a new relationship with God in Jesus Christ. If the urban congregation is to be an agent of such a gospel, it must find ways to model the pluralism of the city in its life.

Treasure: Captive to a Transforming Christ

If the churches are captive to cultural forces, their call is to become captive to the Christ who transforms every culture. Churches, as human institutions, reflect their culture. But they embody divine reality also. Churches are to *become* the church of Jesus Christ. How?

Centering on a new mission consciousness. Our cultural context demands a new Christian commitment from the church. Both the successes and the aging of our structures call for a renewal of mission commitment within our churches. Success dims purpose and aging can diminish one's enthusiasm for accepted purposes. Until there is a renewal of allegiance to the mission of Jesus Christ as central to all the churches, we can be little more than waterless wells and empty vessels of culture religion, mouthing pious platitudes and screaming lifeless rhetoric. Carl Braaten has written, "The flaming center of the Christian message is Jesus, the Christ of God, the Savior of mankind and the Lord of history. Our overriding concern is to remind the church of its task to proclaim this message to all the nations until the end of history."[14]

Is there some demonstration within the world culture of this reality? Yes, it is the focus of the churches upon the needs of persons. The theology of the gospel is a call to focus upon the hurts of humanity by binding up the wounds of the lonely traveler set upon by thieves (Luke 10:25-37). Jesus inaugurated his ministry upon the foundation of an emancipation proclamation of an exiled minority who believed in a God of deliverance. His declaration of intent was to preach good news to the poor, to proclaim release to the captives and recovery of sight to the blind, to set at liberty the oppressed, and to proclaim the reality of a permanent jubilee year (Luke 4:18-19). This manifesto focuses upon persons. The whole gospel is the continuing account of the Lord moving in and out of the masses to lay the hand of healing, release, sight, and liberation upon the hurting persons about him. If Jesus is to be the transforming Lord of the church, that same attention to persons must be the shape of its presence in the world.

Critiquing the self-centeredness of materialism. A second requirement of the churches becoming captive to Christ is to become prophetic. A church which has no judgment to render upon its culture has no courage. There is no greater barrier to the fulfillment of Jesus' mission than the materialism of our age. Americans have been and are captive to economics as perhaps no other people in history. Tocqueville wrote, "I know no other country where love of money has such a grip on men's hearts."[15] This has not changed in the 150 years since he wrote.

A commitment to urban mission will be an expensive commitment. Doing church in the city requires more expense in the form of property and buildings, adequately paid personnel, specialized communication media, and services of care for the poor than for rural contexts. A sacrificial giving to programs of urban ministry are demanded if the benefits of a material culture are to be transformed into the light of Christ's treasure.

Constructing a vision of kingdom commitment. The call of Jesus is to obedience in his kingdom. If the churches are to become agents of a transforming gospel on mission in the city, they must focus priority upon the kingdom. The church is not the goal of Christian mission. Rather, the kingdom of God is the standard by which the church must measure its effectiveness. The kingdom judges the church. It rejects violence and its consequences. The kingdom is the rule of God where sin is forgiven, the status of rich and poor is revised, suffering is alleviated, and God is praised continually. It is a future vision but also a present possibility. It is what we are to preach and teach. It is the city which is to come.

Churches in cultural captivity do not have the biblical vision of that which is coming. But they can have. Members of the earthen vessels within which the treasure of the gospel is contained, often hidden, must look for and work for future reality. That is why Jesus taught his disciples to pray, "Thy kingdom come, Thy will be done, On earth as it is in heaven" (Matt. 6:10, RSV).

Notes

1. H. Richard Niebuhr, *Christ and Culture* (New York: Harper and Brothers, 1951).

2. James M. Gustafson, *Treasure in Earthen Vessels: The Church as a Human Community* (New York: Harper and Row, 1961).

3, Heinrich Schlier, "Eleutheros," *Theological Dictionary of the New Testament*, Vol. II, ed. by Gerhard Kittel, trans. and ed. by Geoffrey W. Bromiley (Grand Rapids: Wm. B. Eerdmans, 1964), p. 496.

4. C. Kirk Hadaway, "A Compilation of Southern Baptist Churches and Resident Members Located in Standard Metropolitan Statistical Areas," unpublished report (Atlanta: Home Mission Board, 1979).

5. Jackson W. Carroll, Douglas W. Johnson and Martin E. Marty, *Religion in America: 1950 to the Present* (New York: Harper and Row, 1979).

6. The Gallup Organization, Inc., *The Unchurched American* (Hopewell, N.J.: Princeton Religion Research Center, 1978) and J. Russell Hale, *The Unchurched: Who They Are and Why They Stay Away* (San Francisco: Harper and Row, 1980).

7. Quoted in Elmer Duncan, *Soren Kierkegaard* (Waco: Word Books, 1976), p. 26.

8. Carroll, Johnson, and Marty, pp. 8-35.

9. Martin E. Marty, "Dangerous Future or Quiet Turning," *Home Missions* 51:62 (July-August, 1980).

10. *Religion in America 1979-80* (Hope, N.J.: Princeton Religion Research Center, n.d.), pp. 8, 26, 29.

11. Carl S. Dudley, *Where Have All Our People Gone? New Choices for Old Churches* (New York: Pilgrim Press, 1979).

12. Jerald B. Bachman, Lloyd D. Johnson, and Patrick M. O'Malley, *Monitoring the Future: Questionnaire Responses from the Nation's High School Seniors* (Ann Arbor: Institute for Social Research, The University of Michigan, 1980), p. 18.

13. Benjamin A. Reist, *Theology in Red, White, and Black* (Philadelphia: Westminster Press, 1975), p. 24.

14. Carl E. Braaten, *The Flaming Center: A Theology of the Christian Mission* (Philadelphia: Fortress Press, 1977), p. 2.

15. Alexis de Tocqueville, *Democracy in America*, ed. by J. P. Mayer, trans. by George Lawrence (Garden City: Doubleday and Co., 1969), p. 54.

5

Our Urban Future
Orrin D. Morris

What will our urban future be? Will the big city be a safe place to live? Will there be harmony among neighborhoods? Will jobs be plentiful so that everyone who wants to work can? Will churches thrive in the big city? Will there be less crowding and better housing? Will we be able to travel freely about the city for work and pleasure? Will the environment be healthy? Will there be adequate medical facilities and skilled personnel?

These are legitimate questions to raise about our urban future. The answers are not definite; they will depend greatly on the kind of future city residents want. If we as city dwellers in AD 2000 want a city with all the positive qualities, we must dream and lay plans to make that dream a reality. We may think of the future in terms of push-button leisure. Generally, such fantasies are the product of daydreams; but what we need is creative, serious, problem-solving dreaming. Creative dreaming is the subject of this chapter.

We will be traveling to the city of Metropolis located somewhere in the United States in 2001. We will not go there just once, as if there might be only one possible future, but we will visit Metropolis four times. Each visit will offer a different scenario—a totally different possibility.

Before we visit Metropolis, some rationale for scenarios is needed. Since the future does not exist, it must be invented. It must be created as a mental picture or dream. The scenario is one method of creating a mental image or description of a possible future. Planners might use this same technique on a large construction project. However, as the planner would employ an architect's drawing, we will employ a verbal sketch. When the processes used by engineers on a large project are studied, three elements are discovered that help us think about the future: (1) the interconnectedness of a wide range of decisions, (2) the crucial importance of time, and (3) the importance of bringing ideas into focus. Watch for these elements during interviews on our Metropolis visits.

Listen to words and understand feelings. Grasp the trends that led to this year of AD 2001, and observe how changes were incorporated and perceptions were modified. Listen as dreams past and present are verbalized. There may be many things you would like to ask, but do not interrupt. At the end of each visit, we will reflect on some things you have heard.

The first visit will be with Robert Harris. He has been selected as a typical Sunday School teacher in a large city. Our visit takes place in his home in Metropolis on Sunday afternoon, February 18, 2001. You are seminary students who are going to hear about the significance of technology in the urban church.

Metropolis—A Fantasy World of Technology

"They still call me a teacher at our church. The name that is recommended is 'facilitator,' but some of us are slow to change. Slow? That's not a fair evaluation. Actually our church is not as slow as some, especially those in the country. Did you know there are some rural churches today that are no further advanced than we were in the late 1970s? Two weeks ago I attended a teleconference for church-school facilitators. During one of the breaks, I communicated with a pastor of one of those rural churches. He said some things that caused me to do a lot of thinking. But you did not come to hear me think. You want to know how we operate our Sunday School.

"The pupils' bus arrives at 9:42, but because it takes at least five minutes to get the facilitator console and terminals set up, I have to arrive at 9:37. When the youth finally settle into their chairs, I activate the enhancement discs with my facilitator console. These hold Scriptures, the entire Bible no less, various illustrations for the lesson, and other teaching, I mean, facilitation aids. While I'm doing that, the students arrange and test their interactive spectrum terminals. This morning our study was on

Matthew 20. I chose to focus on the meaning of greatness in the kingdom and used four dramas. I started with the drama of Zebedee's wife begging Jesus to choose her sons, James and John, to sit on either side of his throne. While the dialogue progressed, I timed it so that the words of Jesus were shown on their displays—just at the moment he made his initial response—I think it was verse 22.

"My pupils know that when I stop the action I'm going to make a special point later. I like to use the King James text. It is located on the Scripture storage disc of my facilitator console. I think there are fourteen different versions of the Bible on the disc—but I use the King James Version most often.

"I let the drama resume until it reached the discourse by Jesus. At the very end of the discourse, I stopped the action again, superimposed the text for verses 27-28, and let the drama play until it was completed. At each stop, the pupil has the option to store the text in the memory of their terminals for later recall, change it to a different translation, or to ignore it.

"The next step in this morning's lesson was the vignettes from the illustration storage disc—there were many of these stored on the disc, but I used 114, 22, and 87. Each was rich in meaning. In case you are not familiar with these, they are brief visual dramas of adult role models with which the youth can identify. The latest version of the illustration disc was transmitted February 2, 2001 from the Sunday School Board. This new version not only has the actor's dialogue that can be superimposed on the displays at stop-action points but it also has the synthesized voice of the actor's inner thoughts. We can follow along as the actors subverbalize what they think. We hear the plotting and scheming or the evaluation and rationalization. If I prefer, I can revise any part of the dialogue and also alter lip movements.

"At this point in the lesson, the teaching fun really begins. I blanked all the terminals and flipped my console into the interactive mode. As I asked a question verbally, the console translated the words into text on the pupils' terminals. Next, I activated their wands. If you have not seen one of these, let me explain that they are sort of like electric pencils with which to mark on their terminals. This way the pupils can interact with the console, writing in new dialogue or responding to screen prompts.

"In the class this morning, I asked them to change the outcome of illustration 114. Chan, Abdul, and Mary created excellent substitutes. I could view each on my console's display, but today Fernando ventured a response. He's my only deaf pupil, and this was about the third time he's attempted a response. I signaled for his permission—he gave it. I always let the pupil decide if the rest of the class will get to see his substitute dialogue or subverbal remarks. Fernando's creation (that's what we call the substitutions) made Mark, the DNA researcher, become very aggressive—he seemed to want to dominate the scene, a laboratory encounter with a Botswana doctor.

"I think we saw how Fernando felt about himself in the substitution. Several of the class members probed the application of the summary verses. Fernando's response was amazing. He seemed to grasp how fiercely competitive he had become trying to compensate for a felt deficiency, his deafness.

"Of equal significance to the class was the other pupils' empathy with Fernando's 'isolation' from the verbal world.

"I get very excited about this technology. There are so many more improvements that will be on the market for churches soon. I know because they are being tested in private schools right now. That's one of the many technological advantages of living in a big city—we get it first.

"But I have an uneasy feeling. I used to not think about it until I communicated with the pastor of the country church. You see, we get a fresh transmission via satellite from the Sunday School Board *every* month. I don't mean my church gets the transmissions—the city associational office does. That's another exciting part of living in Metropolis. The association has the facilitator-training messages on a twenty-four-hour dial-up system. My home-communicator set—a combination of TV, computer, teletype, and telephone—is old, but I can record messages very quickly. This allows me to play back the messages at any time.

"I can't forget the pastor out in the country, a town in Southern Iowa, I think. Perhaps we could take an offering to help his association get a receiving dish—then they could transmit to their churches too.

"Well, I hope this discussion has helped you write your evaluation report for the seminary. Allow me one other word—off the record. A teacher I had back in the 1970s taught me something that has stuck with me; the key to effective teaching is the character of the facilitator not the elaborate technology. I'm going to change my mind, you can put that in your report, the facilitator technology is good to have, but it is only as good as the facilitator using it. And you can't use it right if you have not prepared for the lesson." (End of scenario.)

Reflections on Visit 1: You can be certain that the technology society uses in 2001 will be very advanced compared to what is used today. One trend which suggests this conclusion is the fascination of youth with electronic games. The more they play with electronics, the more comfortable they will be with electronic gear in the future. Most of the older generation are shy of computers, but the generation that is coming along will not be. If anything, they will be aggressive with them, the same as your generation was more aggressive with the use of the automobile than your parents' generation.

A second trend that hints of a high-technology future is the expanding of electronics into the daily office operations. Examples of this include word-processing equipment, typewriters with memories, electronic calculators, minicomputers, and automated graphics equipment.

A third trend is the cooperative efforts of denominational agencies to launch churches into the era of low-watt television transmission and expanded cable-TV programming.

Direct reflection on the scenario reveals several other possible trends. Society tends to be increasingly time conscious. Robert Harris had become concerned with milliseconds. High technology could lead to a widening gap in the development between big city and rural, small-town churches.

By far the most important observation we must keep in mind is the personal dimension in the scenario. Robert Harris rambled between a fascination with technology and a concern for persons.

He was sensitive to the needs of his pupils and was conscious of the danger of technological fascination superseding human relationships. Whatever the future might be, you can be sure there will be exciting new technologies. There also will be the danger of the technologies becoming the master.

It is time to visit Metropolis again. We will visit Dr. Alfred Lee, the resident ethnographer on the mayor's staff. He is a member of one of our churches and welcomes us as urban researchers for the denomination. Listen carefully for the creative energy of an idea.

Metropolis—The Pluralistic City

"The 2000 census indicated the population of Metropolis exceeds one million. This represents a 12 percent increase over 1990. We are grateful it was not more rapid because of the other changes. The increase of 110,000 persons does not tell the whole story. We have had 249,000 persons to move away during the decade and almost 360,000 new persons to move into our city. I doubt if we could have absorbed a greater number during the transition without having been faced with anarchy. But we made it, and that's important!

"Metropolis is like many other cities in America today, a mosaic of many cultures. But we are special because many scientists from other cities visit here regularly to learn how we have created such harmony. They talk of plans to follow our accomplishments, but there was something uniquely spontaneous about our experience.

"To give you an idea of how diverse we are, let me quote a few facts from the 2000 census. Hispanics are the most numerous group with 312,000. Most are Mexican-American, but there are 86,000 immigrants from Mexico, 41,000 Cubans, 11,000 Puerto Ricans, and 4,700 Guatemalans. The second largest group is blacks, 287,200. Most blacks are native-born but there are 70,000 Nigerians and 7,500 Zaire refugees. The third largest group is white, native-born Anglos; they number 227,800. Asians number 122,100, including about 16,000 Japanese; 15,000 Chinese; 14,500 Koreans; 14,000 Vietnamese; 13,000 Laotians; 12,700 Cambodians;

11,000 Asian Indians; 10,200 Filipinos; and 8,000 Indonesians. The rest of the Asians are multicultural. Europeans number almost 82,000 but most are second-generation immigrants whose old country roots date back to the midcentury. The one exception is the Poles who came as refugees about fifteen years ago. I think they number almost 7,000. There are many other groups who number fewer than a thousand each—groups like the American Indians, Haitians, Bahamians, and Jamaicans. Our city has become an international trade center of businesspersons with temporary visas from sixty-two countries. We have consuls and attachès from twenty-seven countries. We *are* cosmopolitan and international.

"Now don't think for a moment that Metropolis is racially diverse by accident. There have been at least twenty years of hard work from many groups within the public and private sector. Our pilgrimage toward pluralism really started when several churches became involved in the resettlement of refugees from Southeast Asia. Later, many of these churches helped resettle Cubans, Haitians, Poles, and Guatemalans—all of this occurred between 1977 and 1984. Then came the African crises.

"Anyway, the youth assimilated quickly into the educational system, but not the elders. Several of our community groups observed a strong tendency for these various refugees to cluster in certain sections of town. Of course, shops emerged in these areas, and some social clubs too. When the manufacturing plant and the regional offices of a computer firm located in Metropolis, the leaders from various suburban cities held a series of planning hearings in 1983. These were the same cities that eventually voted to consolidate into Metropolis in 1988. Anyway, we had discovered from the 1980 census that 6 of our largest cities, including the central city, had lost 25 to 34 percent of their middle-class population during the 1970s.

"The hearing uncovered two problems: (1) our cities had become racially polarized, especially whites and blacks pitted against each other and (2) the public ethos was based on competition—winner take all—one of those I-win-you-lose mentalities. We were doing that at our metro commission meetings. This was happening between school districts, among neighborhood groups, and even among churches. Well, to make a long story short, we involved representatives from the area community organizations and asked them to hold area town-hall meetings.

"Somewhere amid the exchanges (and some were bitter) an idea caught on that our society was enriched by all the different nations who were present. We have no idea from where the thought came, but it was there—a creative explosive idea, a powerful motivator. 'Metropolis—the rich city'—then the spin-offs multiplied. The spiritual fabric began to take form: a city where residents were enriched by the many peoples.

"Minorities were no longer second-class participants; they were the main actors. Little Tokyo, Korean Five-Points, Little Djarkarta, New Warsaw, Ciudad Plaza, San Antonio Square, and so on, grew up overnight. The International Mall was designed for downtown, encompassing six square blocks with Central Street dedicated to pedestrians. We accepted foreign investors, and they thought we had a good idea. All this ended most of the middle-class flight and stabilized our neighborhoods.

"The first half of the past decade was the most difficult time. The new ethos was verbalized for three or four years by community leaders, but the critics made fun of the 'liberal verbage' and said they were empty words. The 'rich city' campaign was launched in 1988, but the new values did not begin to guide city affairs until 1990. Life around city hall became very tense when the board of education developed 'rich city' curriculum. They scheduled festivals and special history weeks. Through these events, our children became oriented to the enrichment of our pluralistic society.

"But these were very awkward years. Critics stormed that we were 'brainwashing' innocent children and youth, and that controversy died slowly. Everything was unnatural. I say it was unnatural because we mouthed words of the new ethos but were scared it wouldn't work unless there was a lot of 'syrup'—you know what I mean—we overdid everything. I'm about to conclude that's the way change frequently comes, we structure an ideal, then we act as if it were real and finally it becomes second nature.

"I could go on and on about the massive infusion of money, the new industries, the redesign of suburban commercial centers, and even the out-migration of some outraged citizens. And I have some great stories about the wealthy elites who threatened financial boycotts and their reactions to restrictive zoning laws. But you get the picture—it is not an uncommon sequence of events.

"As you know, I'm an active Southern Baptist. And the exciting thing is to see how pluralistic our churches have become. At least one out of every three is as pluralistic as their side of the city. The others are monocultural like most of the neighborhoods—and that's OK. But the associational meetings are the most beautiful sights and sounds you've ever witnessed.

"As a black, I had been caught up in a fierce competitive and humanistic mind-set. But when I realized that I was racist in my own attitudes, the reconciliation with my brothers in other races began to happen rapidly. Now I can be a person in Christ, a person who happens to be black. Though I started by quoting figures on the various groups, we are all foremost Metropolites—persons with a particular heritage with which we enrich one another." (End of scenario.)

Reflections on Visit 2: Dr. Alfred Lee owned a piece of a dream—a very powerful dream that was becoming a reality. Did you note the time frame? Change does not happen overnight nor is it without great costs. But there is a principle to be noted when talking about the future—we have a lot more power over our future than most people realize. We do not have to be victimized by impersonal forces but in profound ways can mold our urban future.

Our third trip to Metropolis is a bittersweet journey. Listen carefully and with compassion. Much of what you hear will speak of the bad side of society—but listen also to the good side. All changes have both—the bad from one perspective may be the good for others. I have arranged for you to meet Reginald Brown, the mayor of Metropolis since 1988.

Metropolis—The Island City

"They say we are still losing population but all our people have never been counted. Perhaps we have lost some—it doesn't matter. It never has mattered because there are more than a million people in Metropolis and that's more than most cities. We may be poor, but we're poor, black, and proud. And you know, there are a hundred big cities in America that are poor, black, and proud.

"Our population is not all black for we have more than 10,000 Mexican-Americans and probably 50,000 whites. A lot of these people are elderly. Times have really been bad for everyone, and a lot of folk can't make it without some assistance. I would rather call it assistance than welfare because nobody can fare well on the small amount received. There's little justice in a system that lets the rich get richer and the poor get poorer.

"I think our future is going to be better than our past—at least better than the past twenty years. We have a large number of young men who are ready to work. The high birthrate in the 70s and 80s has given us a larger proportion of young men than other races. These men will be needed by industry and by every sector in the economy. In the past, our young people walked the streets looking for jobs, but friends, the 'jobs are going to be walking the streets' to find our young—you watch what I say.

"I know you want me to talk about the past, but I hate to look back because bitter memories can poison the spirit. However, since you insist, let me set the record straight because all the negative things you have heard about the decay in the cities aren't true. We have gained a lot of power compared to what we had in the old days.

"Metropolis has gone through a series of changes. We lost about 300,000 whites in the 1970s and that many or more in the mid-1980s. When the mortgage money began to loosen up in the mid-1980s they ran—can you imagine—they ran like rats leaving a sinking ship. But look around. Have we sunk? No! And we are not going to either.

"The flight of these people was bad and it was good. It was bad because we were not prepared to cope with the loss of their taxes. It was bad because many of our people became very discouraged.

"But there is always the other side of every coin. It was good for the community leaders who decided that if we were going to make it we were going to have to depend on ourselves. It was good because many neighborhoods felt harmony rather than racial strife eating at their hearts. It was good for our black industries, black banks, and black businesses. It was good for business when many African nations realized we knew where we were going and how to get there.

"Now let me go to the heart and be honest with you. Metropolis had been plagued by racism built right into all the structures of city life. We had no power until 'The Movement' started. We became aware that we could be heard, and there was power in the streets. We then took our power to the voting booth. As our power grew, some of the people moved—if they couldn't have it all, they wouldn't have any.

"Even thousands of Mexicans moved when they found we weren't going to hold classes in two languages in the schools. There was no way we could afford to do something like that—so they 'moved on.' Can you imagine what it would have cost for two sets of teachers and two sets of books? If people are going to be Americans they ought to speak English.

"But if there weren't enough trouble already, we had a protest group of Chinese who used to live here. They made a lot of demands about schools too. Would you believe it? They acted as if everyone who graduated from high school had to be ready to go to Harvard. We tried to work it out, but there was no way to satisfy them. They were good people, but there was no way to make them happy.

"I guess the thing that really hurt the most was what some of our own people did when they moved away. Now there weren't as many to move away as the sensational headlines declared. I guess they got their fancy college degrees from white schools and wanted to live like whites. I didn't mean to say it that way, but right when we were getting everything worked out, off they went. Off they went to the fancy new houses in the country. Off they went to let us rot! But we didn't. We survived, not only survived, but we now have a strong and proud city. You know something? You will give up if you don't keep looking for the bright side.

"You wanted to know about our churches, too, didn't you? They are doing well. We have our own strong associations and conferences. Our pastors help us at city hall too. They know what's going on in the streets, and they help keep everything in harmony.

And I'll tell you another thing about our churches. They don't turn their backs on the old folk—old whites, old Mexicans, old folk who still live in the neighborhood. Those churches look after them because it's right—the right thing to do—even if the old folk's kin in the country forget them. We won't forget them because I guess they are sort of like we are—kind of ignored—but it won't be for long." (End of scenario.)

Reflections on Visit 3: Look about you today. How many persons do you know who are moving farther away from the city? How many do you know who are moving back to the city? What will happen in the mid-1980s when mortgage money becomes more available and the middle class moves from the central cities? Dr. Alfred Lee gave us one view of our urban future when he described the pluralistic city. However, the bittersweet description by the Honorable Reginald Brown could be the urban future of many cities of the East and South. Unless the hearts of many people of all races are changed, a bittersweet future awaits us. The hope is in the gospel of Christ, for there is no other power available to give humanity a new heart.

The fourth and final visit to Metropolis provides us insight into the power of technology to alter many structures of society. For example, when the automobile was mass produced, cities began to spread into the suburbs and beyond. In this final visit, we will interview Frank Hutchinson who is director of the regional planning commission. We will describe life in Metropolis as a result of several unusual crises, all related to the energy needs of a large thriving megalopolitan area. Many different energy sources are being tapped because petroleum, though plentiful, has been dedicated to a narrow sector of the economy.

Metropolis—The Energy Conscious City

"Welcome to Energy City, USA. That is what we're trying to become. As you can see, we are not the compact city many thought. The compact city was a good model for the Europeans, but it won't work for us today. We are a 'low altitude' city, and soon there won't be an apartment more than three stories tall or an office building more than four stories. Metropolis encompasses about 24,000 square miles. From the city center we reach 40 miles north, 80 miles south, 80 miles east, and 120 miles west.

"Our average housing unit contains about 1,400 square feet of living space. Each new unit is carefully designed to include solar cells on the roof. Most units have hydroponic greenhouses in which to grow fresh vegetables. With these stipulations, housing must be spread out—it cannot be stacked vertically.

"In a few years there will not be any rural area left in America. All residential development will be within designated urban areas—an interconnected network of urban developments. There will be many ranges of residential density but no unit will be allowed to occupy more than five acres of land.

"About five years ago, every inch of land in the United States was zoned into the general categories: urban, industrial, agricultural, and recreational. The urban zones allow for offices, retail businesses, and six densities of residential development.

"Buffer zones have been developed between agricultural and industrial areas. Nuclear plants and waste disposal facilities are located there. In the buffer between recreational and residential areas, the original plan called for the relocation of all cemeteries. This has become an explosive issue. Even most churches which supported a comprehensive plan of energy conservation opposed this policy.

"Let me give you a little background. Petroleum was scarce, then became abundant, then scarce again—a cycle that this nation has experienced since the 1920s. The peaks occurred in the late 20s and the late 60s and the mid-80s. The lows occurred in the early 40s, the mid-70s, and the 90s. Each period of scarcity (whether by war, a petro cartel, or the recent Third World Rebellion) was followed by new efforts to discover petro reserves. However, each new wave of exploration resulted in the doubling or tripling of prices.

"The Third World Rebellion was a complex crisis, but the spark that set it off was the new round of price hikes imposed by the exporters—mainly the USA and the USSR. This is where the churches got involved. Most of the churches were very sympathetic toward the complaint of the developing nations that "we can never develop if those who have an abundance of petro export it at inflated prices.' Anyway, you know the story of the various raw materials included in the boycotts and the terrorist threats—the nuclear blackmail. We had begun to recycle everything that could be recycled, but we couldn't survive a nuclear war. Thus the developed nations capitulated with considerable changes in export and import policies. The churches were prime movers in developing global stewardship themes. They were the strong advocates of a sane policy of resource conservation and global community—and now they are after the planners with a vengeance.

"Our Blue Sky ordinance was a direct result of the support from the churches. When engineers demonstrated that elevators consumed twenty times as much energy as was required to heat a skyscraper in the dead of winter—and that the amount of steel and concrete required to reach upward could provide five times as much square footage of horizontal construction—down came the church people. They marched on city hall; they marched on the planning commission; they marched on the White House. So now we issue no building permits for structures over four stories high and only special lifts for handicapped persons are allowed. The churches were prime movers, but now they are after us again.

"Microelectronics permits communication networks that have practically eliminated the need for high density business activities. As we assessed the areas of wasted space, we began by eliminating the downtown parking spaces—one half of all downtown space was used for autos in 1990. Now, we have mass transit in underground tubes that move the public at one thousandth of the cost of ten years ago. The next big waste space were the ribbons of highways. They have been replaced by electronically controlled accessways for modern vehicles. They require only a six-foot right-of-way. The third big barrier to development—I dare not say a waste of space— were the cemeteries.

"I'm an active church member, but I cannot understand the priority that is put on the dead at the expense of the living. But this issue will have to be resolved by the commissioners. I'm glad I do not have to make that decision. I also hope it will be a cloudy day when the commissioners meet so no protesters will attend.

"Cloudy days are a new kind of problem for us. Metropolis is very dependent on sunshine since petroleum is dedicated to airplane transportation, space vehicles, and national defense. You know, rockets and airplanes can't use coal or electricity. So when there are as many as four consecutive days of clouds, the city shuts down just like we used to do during blizzards or ice storms. We stay at home and reduce the energy consumption. Those industries that must stay in operation are given priority to stored energy. Everything else has to be shut down.

"Businesses are geared to sunlight. In the winter we work from 9:00 to 3:00 o'clock, but in the summer from 7:30 to 5:30. Even churches are not allowed to open at night. For those of us who visit for our church, the evenings are a delightful opportunity. Neighborhood home-fellowships and family religious activities are fairly common. It is interesting to me that we are living in the twenty-first century, but the neighborhood church is more like it was in the mid-twentieth century." (End of scenario.)

Reflections on Visit 4: There are several national and global trends that give credence to this scenario. Most of these trends relate to the values of the American citizen.

The US economy has become increasingly dependent upon foreign imports. This dependency has made the economy vulnerable to rise and fall of the governments of many Third World nations. Our vulnerability will increase in proportion to our blind greed for an inordinate share of the world's resources.

These several trends may lead toward increased militancy or a weakened national will. The scenario implies the latter, with a capitulation to the nuclear blackmail of terrorists. While Americans seem to grope about for meaning, a growing restlessness can be noted among many Third World nations. On one hand, the restlessness is rooted in a growing awareness of the power that is inherent in having valuable natural resources that industrialized nations need. On the other hand, the restlessness is rooted in expectations raised by the widely distributed images of Western affluence.

Conclusion

Our four trips to Metropolis have taught us that there are many possible futures for American cities. However, we observed several important principles that should help us as we approach the future. First, *the future does not exist, so it must be invented.* Creative dreams can be translated into powerful ideas that greatly influence the future of the cities. Second, *time is important because many decisions that are made now will affect the future.* Third, *all of life is interconnected.* Another child born in India affects the price of groceries in Dallas. A family who moves to Fairbury, Nebraska, affects the tax structure in two cities, the one to which the family moved and the one from which they moved. A person committing himself to faith in Christ, converts to a new set of values which affect all relationships. Fourth, *change is a sign of life.* Some changes are good, but others are bad. In most situations, change is both good and bad, depending upon a person's perspective. Fifth, *the technology that a society employs can have a profound effect on the shape of the city and on the relationships of its citizens.*

Finally, *crises precipitate change, and problems inspire creativity.* Solutions are not always in terms of trend projections. Many times change is introduced as a leap forward or a step sideways, onto a preferred course. I feel it is accurate to predict that the church will survive quite well in the midst of change, offering the "message of hope."

Edward B. Lindaman summed up the Christian perspective of the future best when he wrote:

> In Christ we have been given the gift of commitment to the future; the power of God is in our midst. And we are free to stand before eternal possibilities to transcend the present. In Christ, the promises of God—the future of God—are confirmed and validated *but not yet completely fulfilled.*

For me to think in the future tense is to join in God's great and good Creation, seeing in hope an affirmation of the importance of my participation, my love.[1]

Let us face the future—our urban future—with a sense of mission to dream the dreams that will make our cities a part of "God's great and good creation."

Note

1. Edward B. Lindaman, *Thinking in the Future Tense* (Nashville: Broadman Press, 1978), p. 180.

6

The Church in the Urban Setting
C. Kirk Hadaway

The greatest problems and the greatest possibilities for churches exist in the cities; for here we find the fastest growth, the largest churches. But here we also find the most rapid decline and the easiest death. One look at the churches highlighted in Elmer Towns's *The Ten Largest Sunday Schools*[1] reveals that all are urban churches. It takes a large city to produce a Crystal Cathedral with 11,000 members, or First Baptist Church, Dallas with 23,000. Urban centers allow such "super churches" to emerge through the sheer numbers of available Christians in each denomination and through the easy access made possible by the city's transportation network. Similarly, the fastest growing churches in America also tend to be urban. Decadal growth rates of 50 percent, 100 percent, 200 percent or even 300 percent, which are called respectively, "not too bad," "in pretty good shape," "newsworthy," and "very significant" by church growth writers,[2] can only be sustained in urban areas. After all, in rural communities, a church growing this rapidly would soon run out of possible converts.

The unfortunate reverse of the rapid growth and massive size which the city makes possible is the precariousness which many churches find in urban neighborhoods. As racial transition begins, some churches find their membership dropping so rapidly that they virtually have no chance to recover. In cities across America, many churches of all denominations have closed. Some have slowly dwindled until they could no longer afford to heat the building, while others went from healthy growth to rapid decline almost overnight. The problem is so serious in the Atlanta area that in the two most populous counties there was a net loss of thirty churches among Southern Baptists alone between 1970 and 1980. Similar losses in churches have been suffered by Methodists in Memphis, Presbyterians in Chicago, and by various denominations in a host of other cities.

What is it about the city which produces the boom-or-bust nature of the church? To find the answer, we have to look at the structure of the local church in America and at the setting of the church in American cities.

The Local Church in American History

The Protestant church emerged as an institution serving a local parish. In our colonial period, the parish was typically a growing but cohesive local community with fairly definite geo-graphical boundaries.[3] As long as the community survived, the church remained viable because, by nature, it was *part* of the local community. New residents added to the population and replaced those who died, moved, or went to war; but by and large the social characteristics of the residents changed very slowly. Also, residents had very little choice in where they went to church and disgruntled members did not have the option of breaking away and forming a new congregation. A person who lived in the parish attended the parish church or, more likely, did not attend at all. And even if the latter option was chosen, he was likely to be taxed anyway for the support of the church.

The parish system could have continued indefinitely if states had maintained the granting of religious monopolies. This was not to be however, and there emerged a new invention in America: the "competitive parish," where churches of several denominations could exist in close proximity and compete for members. The competitive parish meant that the continued prosperity of any one church was not ensured because members and new residents had the option of going elsewhere. But in pre-Civil War America, this situation did not create serious problems for the churches. The United States was still a nation of farms and small towns and even the few cities that existed were fairly small. Growth was steady, but it was not convulsive and the locally based autonomous church seemed to fit it well.

Following the Civil War two related events occurred which

changed the structure of American society. Industrialization and massive immigration acted jointly to swell the size of American cities and accelerated the process of social change. People from the farms and from Europe flooded into Eastern cities and even changed the Midwestern city Chicago from a small town into a metropolis. In the thirty years between 1860 and 1890, Boston and New York City more than tripled in size and Philadelphia more than doubled.

The urban growth and immigrant waves hit the churches hard in American cities because they initiated the process of rapid neighborhood transition. Speaking of the 1880s, Ahlstrom states:

> Remorselessly the population patterns changed. Buildings deteriorated, factories encroached, old residential areas decayed, tenements arose, peaceful streets became crowded thoroughfares. When the constituency of old "down town" churches moved out into new residential neighborhoods, the church itself often followed, perhaps selling the old building to another congregation composed of immigrants. Later, this church, too, would follow "its people" to some more favorable location.[4]

The situation had not changed when Douglass wrote these passages in 1935:

> Differences in human fortunes suffered by the church's immediate constituencies and changes in these fortunes due to changes in the environment largely control the institutional destinies of each particular church. Where the environment is prosperous and progressive the church can scarcely fail to "succeed." Where it is miserable and deteriorating the church can scarcely avoid failure.
>
> The most crucial of the environmental facts is that modern social changes are so many and so great and that they come so fast as to put unparalleled stress upon the church today.[5]

The situation is essentially the same in the 1980s. America has become an urban society, and the certainty of neighborhood change is the only static pattern.

Church Structure Today

Neighborhood churches today are typically structured as if they still served cohesive parishes rather than mobile, noncohesive, heterogeneous urban communities. The membership of most churches is drawn primarily from neighborhoods within a few miles of the church building, an area considerably larger than the urban parishes when members had to either walk or come by carriage. Yet the principle has not changed. The church considers a certain area its territory and may vigorously resist a new church of the same denomination being planted in its community. When neighborhood churches, such as the ones I describe, are organized they begin with a key group of leaders and workers who form the core of the church. These persons are drawn from nearby neighborhoods, and so the church naturally takes on the class character of the surrounding local community. Also, most new neighborhoods begin with families in the same stage of the life cycle, as well as with the same socioeconomic status. The neighborhood starts out as quite homogeneous, often with a genuine community spirit and unity emerging. New churches develop as residents want a church for *their* neighborhood. Being born as expressions of the local community, the churches, along with local schools and other institutions, swiftly become an integral part of the community.

So in their beginnings, urban neighborhoods in America may resemble the cohesive, stable parishes of the past. Churches are able to capitalize on this situation and grow until the wave of new housing construction passes them by. At this point, the similarity between the modern urban neighborhood and the cohesive local community of earlier days begins to blur. Soon after they are built, urban neighborhoods begin to change, often quickly, sometimes slowly; but change they do until the structure of the local community is radically different from what it was when the neighborhood first developed. The process continues as old residents move and are replaced by newcomers. The neighborhood may change in character many times, undergoing aging, revitalization, racial and ethnic transition, moving from affluence to poverty and, in a few cases, back to affluence.

This change brings problems for the local church because the core group of the congregation resists change in its own structure. It begins as a relatively homogeneous group of people who share similar class status, values, and life-styles. Close-knit friendship groups have developed in the church and informal rules of dress and behavior have emerged. The church has an identity. For many members, the congregation has replaced the cohesive community that once was the local parish.

Newcomers to a community may have difficulty in gaining full acceptance in any church, but the problem is especially difficult when these newcomers are not of the same social class, stage in the life cycle, or do not share the same values and life-styles as the members who make up the core of the church. Even if they want to join, which is not always the case, new residents may feel subtly excluded, ignored, or even rebuffed. What has happened in such a church is that the unity, identity, and community which have given it stability through the years may now lead it to decline. There are no neighborhoods which escape the process of change and churches which attempt to remain the same are doomed to failure.

The situation would be difficult enough if it depended solely on the willingness of core members to accept newcomers. Yet it is often true that the newcomers feel that the present structure and orientation of the church simply does not meet their needs. It may be a church of older persons and the newcomers are young, or it may be a family-oriented church and the newcomers are singles or divorced persons. The staffing, programs, style of worship, dress, music, and Sunday School are all oriented to serving people with their own tastes. Unfortunately, it is rare that the membership of a church in such a situation will recognize the problem because, as they see it, the church is open and friendly. After all, *they* are quite comfortable with the church and its programs, so why shouldn't anyone else?

The typical pattern is for the church to remain the same in its composition while the surrounding neighborhoods steadily change. Many loyal members have, in effect, given up on the local community and moved to newer housing, but they still drive back to the church on Sunday. Over time, a gap develops between the church and its community. Whereas the church once totally reflected the age structure and class character of the local community, now there are differences. And the differences tend to increase. The church remains affluent, while the community becomes poorer; the church building is in good repair, but nearby housing becomes somewhat "seedy." The membership increases in age while the community attracts younger residents. In most cases, a core group of members still live in surrounding neighborhoods; but in the worst situations, nearly everyone has left and only return to their old "parish" for worship services. What was once a community church has become what Schaller calls an "ex-neighborhood church."[6] The lifespan of such churches tends to be very short.

All neighborhoods go through a process in which they become less homogeneous and more heterogeneous. Older neighborhoods of twenty or thirty years are especially likely to have a wide variety of residents. Some neighborhoods, like the one in which I lived in Atlanta, have a mix of very old residents, new families with small children, professionals, blue-collar workers, renters, home owners, and so forth. But the transition of a community in terms of age, income, and the like is a rather slow one. Churches, as a rule, do not adjust well to the change; but they will rarely begin rapid declines which end in the death of the church.

Racial Transition and the Neighborhood Church

Racial transition is another story. In cities where the transition is largely white to black, patterns of "white flight" often develop, and neighborhoods totally change their racial character in as little as three or four years. Yet even if the transition is slower, churches typically lose members at an alarming rate. Members move away, and only a certain percentage are willing to drive back to their old neighborhood church in order to worship. Most join churches near their new homes. Racial transition can normally be predicted years in advance by an observant pastor or planning committee because it is directional, "flowing" over time into areas of similar land use. But it always seems to catch churches by surprise. They may fear it, but rarely do they prepare for it. Many churches simply try to ignore the possibility until it is too late, but others probably would not try to adjust (other than to relocate) even if they knew transition was a certainty beforehand. Doing nothing is the most prevalent strategy among Protestant churches in America.

Members who remain in nearby neighborhoods or who commute back to the church cling to the image of their church as it once was. It is *their* church, and they want it to remain the same as long as possible. In a recent conference for churches in transition, the pastor of a church in a transitional community seemed to be desperately seeking some justification for *not* reaching the Hispanic and Asian newcomers to his church field. He reasoned that there are still whites here, "so why can't my church be the one to focus on reaching them?" The trouble was, this was exactly what nearly all white churches in the area wanted to do. They decline because they were competing for a dwindling resource.

As racial transition proceeds, the gap between the church and the local community increases greatly because the social barriers between "we" and "they" are much more significant than when newcomers only differ in terms of age, income, or life-style. Some churches, of course, try to reach out to the new residents, but frequently their efforts receive little response, except from children. Such "open" churches fail largely because, while they are willing to accept newcomers, they want to do it on their own terms. They want the church to retain its present flavor and worship style, and the new residents may not feel that it meets their needs. Given the choice of another church to attend, they often ignore the efforts of well-meaning churches which are dominated by members of another race or ethnic group. Radical change is necessary in the identity of a church and new avenues of entry must be developed if the church in transition is ever to become representative of its community again.

The churches which succeed do so by either altering their worship and staff to fit new residents or they create new units in the church with separate worship services for the new racial/language/ethnic group. Of the two strategies, the first is the most difficult and appears to work best for young congregations. The second option is much more prevalent and is working in cities all over the nation. Yet most churches elect to do neither.[7] They move to new neighborhoods where racial or ethnic transition is not yet a problem, or by their own choice they dwindle and die.

The Regional Church Vs. the Neighborhood Church

There has been a wide variety of church typologies developed in recent years to categorize churches in America. Perhaps the best known are those constructed by Ezra Earl Jones and Lyle Schaller.[8] All of these schemes are quite useful as techniques to highlight particular problems or advantages which certain churches have in common. I do not want to create a new typology. Instead, I want to suggest that one of the most basic structural differences between urban Protestant churches is the extent to which their membership is dispersed.

It is possible to conceive of churches on a continuum ranging from very localized to highly dispersed. The small neighborhood church which draws 90 percent of its members from within a half mile is an extreme on one end of the continuum and the downtown first church which draws from the entire city is the extreme on the other. We might label churches which are largely localized, *neighborhood churches,* and churches which are quite dispersed, *regional churches.*

By far the largest majority of churches in American cities tend to be neighborhood based. In fact, the proportion may be well over 90 percent. As has been described, these churches grow along with surrounding neighborhoods and suffer when the character of these neighborhoods change.

Regional churches are few and far between because they must be *exceptional* for some reason. They may be "special purpose" churches, such as a deaf church, a liturgical Southern Baptist church, an ecumenical avant-garde church, a "recreation church," or a church which represents a very small ethnic population. Also, they may be prestigious, downtown, "old first" churches. Some regional churches do not, of course, draw from the entire city. There are suburban regional churches which draw from very large segments of the metro area because of their location near interstates, large recreational facilities, and exceptional preaching. However, most are not accessible enough to draw from the entire city.

Regional churches are often lifted up as exceptions to the rule that, "as goes the neighborhood, so goes the church." And it is true, this type of church is much less affected by neighborhood change than is the neighborhood church; and the extent of this independence increases as the area from which the church draws its membership also increases. Because of the success of regional churches in many cities, struggling congregations are often told they must emulate these churches if they ever want to grow.

But all churches cannot be regional congregations. The reason is that regional churches must have some exceptional feature which makes it worthwhile for persons to drive eight, ten, fifteen, or even more miles in order to worship in them. All churches cannot be exceptional. There is only a need for a few "special purpose churches," and the supply of truly exceptional preachers is quite limited.

Regional churches may be less dependent upon their environments than are neighborhood churches, but *they are only able to maintain this independence by remaining exceptional.* For example, an inner-city church of 12,000 members cannot afford to have a poor preacher. If it did, a large number of its constituents would not feel the drive to the inner city was worthwhile. At that point, the environment would quickly catch up with the church and it would decline. This is the reason many downtown churches have died. Their memberships have traditionally been dispersed throughout the city; when they ceased being exceptional enough to justify long drives from affluent neighborhoods, they began to decline in membership.

The typical church in America remains a neighborhood-based institution; and while some neighborhood churches draw from a larger area than others, this semiregional nature only mediates the influence of the changing environment to a very limited extent. Our churches minister today in large "competitive parishes" and are structured as if we were still a small-town, agrarian society.

Urban Structure and Church Growth

Cities in America generally have quite similar structures and patterns of growth. For this reason urban churches share similar problems (and similar advantages). Each church environment is, of course, somewhat unique, but the uniqueness is overshadowed by the great similarity to thousands of urban churches across America.

Cities normally will have a center core, or central business district which is surrounded by a somewhat dilapidated area of industry, poor housing (often slums), hospitals, and land leveled by urban renewal. In some cities this "zone of transition" will also contain a few revitalized sections with rehabilitated older homes or high-rise apartments and condominiums.

Beyond this zone we move into an area of older homes. Some are beginning to fall into disrepair, others are in quite good condition. In many cities, a large portion of these older homes will be occupied by minorities; but in most cities, there will remain stable sections of large, expensive homes, white ethnic enclaves, and areas which are being revitalized by young professionals.

Bands of newer housing surround the old and are generally divided into broad sectors of wealthy, moderate, and working-class homes. Beyond the "newer homes" and normally separated from the city proper by interstate loops, rivers, or industrial tracts are the suburbs. Some of these are fairly old but others are just beginning to be developed. Typically, suburban development is spotty, with areas of farm land, airports, and so forth between suburban communities. Certain suburbs will form around village centers, retaining a townlike structure as they are developed. Beyond the suburban ring will be towns and villages that are economically dependent on the city to some degree.

In Figure 3, it can also be seen that some cities are composed of more than one central business district. A few have no additional city centers; but other cities, like the Los Angeles/Orange County urban sprawl, may have many. In fact, Los Angeles has so many central business districts that downtown Los Angeles is much smaller than would be expected for such a large metropolitan area.

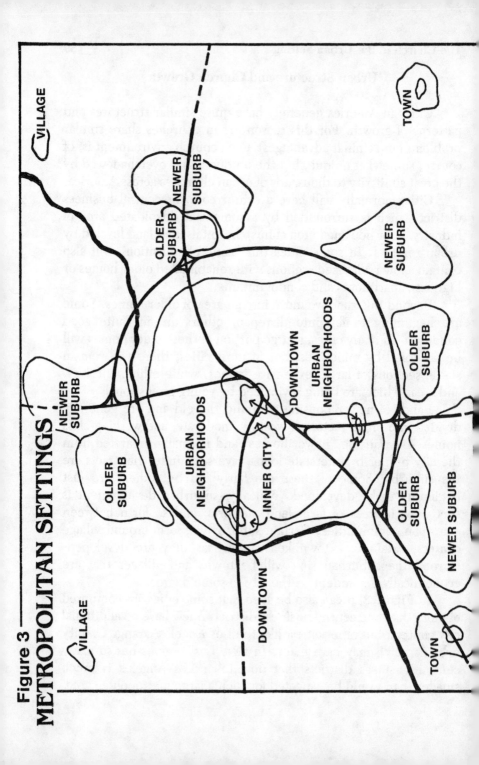

Figure 3
METROPOLITAN SETTINGS

VILLAGE

VILLAGE

TOWN

TOWN

OLDER SUBURB

NEWER SUBURB

NEWER SUBURB

NEWER SUBURB

NEWER SUBURB

OLDER SUBURB

OLDER SUBURB

OLDER SUBURB

URBAN NEIGHBORHOODS

URBAN NEIGHBORHOODS

DOWNTOWN

DOWNTOWN

INNER CITY

Cities also grow in relatively similar fashion. They expand outward from the edges as new neighborhoods are built on farmland or other vacant ground. Each zone within the city also expands over time. The central business district slowly takes over areas of the transitional zone, older homes fall into disrepair, newer homes age, and suburbs grow together. The process is not always quite this simple—zoning affects where housing and businesses can be built, as does the type of land available—but, by and large, cities grow and change in a quite similar manner.

How does urban structure and patterns of urban change affect the growth and decline of churches in American cities? The answer is that it affects churches in different cities and of different denominations in remarkably similar ways.

I have conducted studies of the churches in six diverse cities which represent all regions of the contiguous forty-eight states with the purpose of discovering which factors in the city environment had the most impact on the church. Looking at churches in a variety of mainline denominations, *I found population change to be the most important influence.*[9] In parts of the city where the population was increasing, the churches tended to increase; where population was declining, the churches tended to decline. Such a finding was hardly surprising since all church planners know that churches tend to grow well in expanding suburbs and fare poorly in the declining inner city. Still, I was surprised by the *strength* of the relationship. In some cities, this one fact was enough to predict whether the large majority of churches were either growing or declining.

The second most important factor was racial transition. Housing discrimination in America is such that racial and ethnic minorities tend to be segregated into ethnic enclaves or ghettos, as they are sometimes described. When the population of such groups begins to expand beyond the limits of available housing in their own neighborhoods, members of the racial group will begin to expand its limits by moving into adjacent neighborhoods where few, if any, ethnic persons had lived before. If the growth of the racial/ethnic population is quite rapid and if patterns of "white flight" develop, the boundaries of the ethnic community may expand greatly in a relatively short period of time. During the 1970s in the South, for instance, large areas of lower middle-class and working-class white housing changed completely from white to black. White churches in the path of extensive racial transition tend to decline severely and many die.

Obviously, however, in many cities there is not a large non-white minority component and the limited expansion of such a population would have only a small impact. So the influence of racial transition tends to vary greatly from city to city. In cities like Memphis, where there is a very large black population, the influence of racial transition was close in strength to that of population change. But in cities like Omaha, where racial minority groups are much smaller, the influence was not nearly as great.

Other environmental influences which have been shown to be significant for the urban church are *income levels, educational levels,* and the *percentage of young children* in a community. White, mainline churches tend to fare better in middle-class areas of the city. Middle-class persons are the typical constituency of mainline denominations, so it stands to reason that the greater the percentage of such persons, the more likely are churches to grow. Similarly, white, middle-class areas with a high percentage of young children also tend to be productive for the typical mainline church. As Clark Roof notes:

> Religious involvement is related to the family life cycle with a peak in institutional activity occurring during the parenting phase when children are in the home. Most (families) want their children to have religious instruction, and they are apt to affiliate, or reaffiliate as is often the case, with a church or synagogue out of a feeling of responsibility to participate in the institution to which they send their children.[10]

Many other factors—in addition to population change, racial/ ethnic transition, income, education and age structure—affect the church in the city. Commercial development in residential areas, zoning changes, and highway construction which creates barriers between neighborhoods are just a few more. When all these influences are added together, it reveals the tremendous impact of the environment on the local church.

Church Growth by Location

The churches in various parts of the city are affected by different influences. In some sectors, the overall result of these influences is a productive environment for the church. But in others, the environment is not so productive.

For an overall view of how churches are affected by their settings look at Figure 4. This chart shows the percent of churches growing, on a plateau, and declining in each sector of Memphis, Tennessee. The trend is quite clear: membership growth is very unlikely in the areas closest to downtown and becomes progressively more likely as we move outward to the suburbs.[11]

Downtown and Inner-City Churches

If we look specifically at the downtown and inner-city churches we can see that, at least in Memphis, none of the former and only 10 percent of the latter are growing. The situation in other cities is similar; in the Northeast and Midwest, it is much worse. Jones and Wilson report that in seventy-nine cities, seven out of ten downtown, old First United Methodist Churches lost members between 1960 and 1973.[12]

The problems suffered by downtown and inner-city churches are closely tied to the general decline of the central city across America. Revitalization attempts not withstanding, the central business district declined in prestige, vitality, appearance, and as the center for retail trade. If people, and especially middle-class white people, rarely venture downtown for other reasons, they are not likely to attend church there.

Suburban expansion and the economic decline of older neighborhoods has meant that the typical constituents of mainline churches have farther and farther to drive if they wish to attend a downtown church. At the same time, the appeal of this area has steadily declined as urban decay and crime have become more prevalent. The churches have also aged and may have somber appearances and hemmed in ones as well, being surrounded by taller buildings.

The situation has put great stress on the downtown and inner-

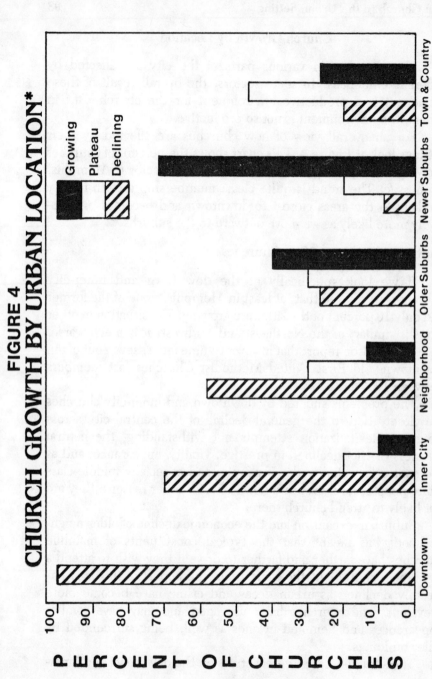

FIGURE 4
CHURCH GROWTH BY URBAN LOCATION*

Growing
Plateau
Declining

Downtown   Inner City   Neighborhood   Older Suburbs   Newer Suburbs   Town & Country

*1970-1980 membership change among all churches of 5 mainline denominations in Shelby County, Tennessee (Memphis). Denominations included Southern Baptist, United Methodist, Presbyterian Church in the United States, and Lutheran Church,

city churches to maintain those exceptional qualities which made them among the largest and most prestigious churches in the city. A few are able to meet the challenge and continue to grow, like First Baptist, Dallas, Texas; but for most, the disadvantages of the downtown location outweigh the appeal of its physical plant, pastor, and program. Decline has slowly set in and is sapping the strength of such churches to maintain their costly buildings and exceptional worship services. And when the quality of worship begins to decline, the once exceptional church may become ordinary. Who wants to drive ten or more miles to an ordinary church when there are vital, active, growing churches nearby? Hardly anyone.

The downtown and inner-city church creates a quite difficult problem for the denomination because it represents both a liability and a largely irreplaceable asset. If such a church closes or moves, the denomination may never be able to establish a viable witness in that area again because of the price of land. At the same time, the downtown church may not be providing much of an active witness to its community anyway, being largely populated by affluent members who drive long distances.

Despite their problems, churches close to the center of the city should be supported in their struggles to remain viable. Ways must be found to provide a ministry to an often deteriorating community and yet to maintain the support of longtime members.

City Neighborhoods

City neighborhoods tend to go through a life-cycle process in which they at first increase and later decline in socioeconomic status relative to newer parts of the city.[13] Some maintain a very high status level, such as the communities of Highland Park in Dallas or Belle Meade in Nashville; but most slowly decline in relative status over time. Of course a life-cycle model also holds the possibility for rebirth or "gentrification," as it is now called; but apparently this happens to relatively few older neighborhoods.

It can be seen in Figure 4 that the churches in city neighborhoods in Memphis are typically either plateaued or declining. Only a few are growing. The same situation is found to be true in other cities.

Many older neighborhoods, especially those closest to the inner city, have long since become dominated by members of various racial and ethnic minorities. Other areas are in the midst of extensive racial transition. In still others, the transition is only beginning. Throughout the city neighborhood area, the population has steadily become more heterogeneous, and most sections also have lost population.

The churches in the city are thus faced with a more heterogeneous population, racial transition, and a decline in their population pool. The result has typically been stagnation and decline. The larger semiregional churches tend to fare better than small neighborhood churches, but for both the situation is quite difficult. Middle-class Protestant families with children in the home are simply shrinking in number, and churches must either do a better job in attracting local residents than when times were good or they will decline. Churches far from the central business district are somewhat more insulated from the problems described above and are likely to remain strong longer. Some churches have been able to accept newcomers with different social and ethnic backgrounds, and a few others have been able to emerge "from the pack" as institutionally exceptional churches and have grown while those around them have not.

So in this broad area of the city, growth is possible but it becomes more difficult each year as neighborhoods age and change in character.

Suburbs

As suburban churches in many cities are now learning, membership growth in the suburbs is not guaranteed. Older suburbs lack open land for future development, and the easy growth which comes with population increase is a thing of the past. Neighborhoods are also beginning to lose their homogeneous flavor and massive black suburbanization in some cities has greatly impacted white suburban churches.

For years suburban churches have subsisted on transfer

growth from the influx of new residents, growth which they generally attributed to their own efforts. But now these churches must face a stable population level and increase their penetration of surrounding neighborhoods if they expect to grow. This is a difficult transition and not all suburban churches are up to it.

Farther out, however, where population growth is still occurring, the churches are booming and building programs are continuous. Some of the churches in these areas are new, others were formerly small-town churches, and still others moved here from "less productive" areas of the city. Most tend to grow, a few have not made the transition from being rural to suburban, and a few managed to fight off the newcomers with internal struggles and by being just plain unfriendly.

As the boundaries of the city expands, each denomination must plant new churches in the developing neighborhoods or lose members to other religious bodies. People usually like to attend churches close to home, and at least for a while these new congregations will have the opportunity for rapid expansion. Suburban churches should be aware, however, that the homogeneous growing neighborhood of today is the heterogeneous declining neighborhood of tomorrow. A few churches may yet become regional or even "super churches," but most will remain neighborhood churches that will hopefully maintain a commitment to ministry among *all* persons who live in the community.

Conclusion

Each church has a setting. It exists at a location, surrounded by streets, houses, shops, and people. This environment affects the church because it depends on nearby residents for its membership but cannot count on them attending. People are not forced to attend any one church or to attend church at all. Where they attend is a very personal decision, based on many subjective factors, not the least of which is their compatibility with and the acceptance they feel from the current membership of the church. After all, new residents are not concerned that the church will suffer by their decision not to join. They are primarily interested in meeting their own personal needs. If the nearest church does not fit the bill, they will go elsewhere or drop out altogether.

Churches are structured both formally and informally to meet the needs of the residents who form their initial memberships. This is natural and to be expected. But neighborhoods change, bringing new residents with new tastes and different needs. Some churches try to adjust but many do not, and even those who make the attempt may not be successful. The decision of which church to join is so personal and there are so many competing alternatives that even very subtle, trivial things may influence prospective members to go elsewhere.

The tremendous impact of a church's setting on membership growth or decline has been demonstrated repeatedly by a tradition of research begun by H. Paul Douglass in the 1920s. Denominational researchers and sociologists in the 1970s have confirmed that the influence remains strong and have even been able to measure the effect relative to other factors impinging on the church. Yet some church planners and church consultants often ignore the influence of the local context, and a few would even deny its importance. How can they make this claim given the overwhelming contrary evidence? The reason may well be found in the relatively unalterable nature of the local context.

A very few exceptional churches have been able to "lift" the character of their neighborhoods, but this is quite unusual. Because so little can be done to alter the context of a church, consultants may feel it is more productive to stress those positive institutional factors in a church which can be improved and the negative factors which can be eliminated. To be sure, it is not simply a changing neighborhood which causes a church to decline; it is the interaction between the setting and the structure of the church—when one no longer fits the other—that causes the decline in membership. So instead of trying to change the unchangeable, a consultant is correct in trying to help a church change *itself*. It should be realized, however, that not any change will do. A church must be changed so that it is attractive to new residents of the community, and this requires an understanding of who they are and why and how the church is either rebuffing them or failing to meet their needs.

If the context did not change, it would not be important, and the church could proceed with its evangelistic business as usual. But the context does change and makes necessary changes in the church itself. To know how to adjust to an inevitably changing environment, each church must first understand the makeup of that environment and how it is changing. Without this knowledge, the church nor its consultant can hope to give an intelligent answer to the question of what a church is to do in the face of membership decline.

There are many options available to the church in the changing community. The most popular is to do nothing. This may prove fatal, but equally risky is the option of a strategy which ignores contextual reality.

Notes

1. Elmer Towns, *The Ten Largest Sunday Schools and What Makes Them Grow* (Grand Rapids: Baker, 1969).
2. C. Peter Wagner, *Your Church Can Grow* (Glendale: Regal Books, 1976), pp. 63-64.
3. Martin E. Marty, *Righteous Empire* (New York: Harper and Row, 1970).
4. Sydney E. Ahlstrom, *A Religious History of the American People* (Garden City: Doubleday, 1975), Vol. II, pp. 193-194.
5. H. Paul Douglass, *The Protestant Church as a Social Institution* (New York: Russell and Russell, 1935), pp. 237-238.
6. Lyle E. Schaller, *Hey, That's Our Church* (Nashville: Abingdon, 1975), pp. 51-68.
7. James H. Davis and Woodie W. White, *Racial Transition in the Church* (Nashville: Abingdon, 1980), p. 59.
8. Ezra Earl Jones, *Strategies for New Churches* (New York: Harper and Row, 1976), pp. 37-42. Schaller.
9. C. Kirk Hadaway, "The Demographic Environment and Church Membership Change," *Journal for the Scientific Study of Religion.* March, 1981, pp. 77-89.
10. Wade Clark Roof, "America's Voluntary Establishment: Mainline Religion in Transition," *Daedalus.* Winter, 1982, p. 174.
11. For further elaboration on the Memphis study see C. Kirk Hadaway, "Church Growth (and Decline) in a Southern City," *Review of Religious Research.* June, 1982.
12. Ezra Earl Jones and Robert L. Wilson, *What's Ahead for Old First Church,* (New York: Harper and Row, 1974), p. viii.
13. Harvey M. Choldin and Claudine Hanson, "Status Shifts Within the City," *American Sociological Review.* February, 1982, pp. 129-141.

7
Evangelizing America's Cities
Dale W. Cross

The nineteenth-century evangelist, Dwight L. Moody, said that the cities of America are the mountain peaks of society. Everything runs downhill from the city; therefore, if we are to reach the nation for Christ we must "strategize" for the cities. Cities are of great significance because of their power in the affairs of the nation and the world. The majority of international trade, the economic exchange, networks for communication, and the originators of social values all center in the cities. But the cities find their greatest role of importance because of the people who live there. More than 70 percent of the total population of America live in metropolitan areas. The massive concentration of minorities, poor, language-culture groups, the elderly, and single persons also give cities unusual significance. The city, the place of such intimidating change, is also the place where Christ would lead his people in rediscovering their purpose on the earth.

Urban Evangelism as Purpose

Our theology, which conceives a purposeful God who calls his creation to collaborate with him in his purpose, must also have a primary urban focus. The Scriptures are clear concerning the purpose of God. God had a dream: a world united, Creator and creature living in harmony. There was serenity in nature, and humans were created for the joyful peace of Eden. Donald Baillie describes this divine intention as a scene around a lively campfire.

> God is a roaring blaze. Humanity is a circle of celebrative dancers, arms linked, facing each other and the light. But the scene is shattered as humanity loves darkness rather than light. The allurement of the night causes each one in the circle to turn around. This

turn breaks the circle of linked arms. Peering out into the darkne~
humanity neither sees the face of his neighbor nor the glow of th
light of God.[1]

"Back-turning" is alienation from neighbor, from nature, and from God. It is the rebellion which the Scriptures call sin and which brings its wages of death to the city streets. The morning newspapers and the evening newscasts saturate our minds with the trauma and troubles of urban America.

There is a tendency during times of social upheaval to avoid the central issues of our back-turning from each other and our rebellion against God's way. We tend to seek a revival of the good old days, the old-time religion. This frequently means calling people back to practices which seemed to be effective in years gone by but which are not responsive to present-day realities. This innocent, often misguided tendency leads to a reestablishment of undesirable, restrictive, and rigid institutionalization, as well as the absolutizing of specific forms and practices which tempt the adherence to bigotry and idolatry. The consequence of this is the missing of the Holy Spirit's response to a new day and forfeiting the renewing power of a new dream.

What shall become of us, we Christians in America, if we continue to celebrate our merging numerical increases while the city masses convulse with a million diseases? What will happen if the leaven and the salt are boxed up and shipped out for safekeeping? Where is the healing if the balm of Gilead is not shared? To those who hunger for meaning, mystery, and mastery in life, we of the church must be ready to respond with the good news of Jesus about life, death, and destiny. There is food for hope-starved hearts, but we must make certain that the bread we offer is not stale or poison to those who receive it.

Dr. Bill Jones of Brooklyn says that evangelism at its best is bringing people into a head-on collision with reality. The city does this to us. The props are kicked out. The facade of religious respectability has been removed. The city lets it all hang out. It was in this kind of environment that Jesus found his most effective witness and in which the first-century church thrived.

The gospel is poisoned whenever the church wears the

culture's values like a well-fitted suit. Yet, in much of America's religious history the church has been fervent in advocating Americanism as the hope of the world. Oftentimes the cross has been so tightly wrapped in the Stars and Stripes that it is hardly recognizable.

The city does not set so comfortably with the myths of American culture. The city is a microcosm of the world, and many urban dwellers have seen this society from the outside looking in. Many of them recognize all too well that the American dream is not the doorway of heaven.

The city offers to Christians the opportunity of presenting the pure gospel as it radically confronts every world system with the announcement that Jesus Christ is Lord. In the city, the battle lines are dramatically drawn. Jacques Ellul has said, "The city historically represents the greatest synthesis of human ingenuity and effort arrayed in rebellion against God."[2] Is it not toward the gates of hell that the church is called to advance? It is in the midst of the battle that we discover who we are and must declare whose side we are really on.

Urban Evangelism as Process

In confronting the task of evangelizing urban America, we must challenge traditional perceptions which see the task as simply dropping evangelistic events into the urban scene. The metropolitan community must be seen as a whole, and strategy processes must be designed which take into account all the peoples of the city and all the concerns which affect the communication of God's good news.

In frequent encounters with church leaders in urban centers, I am continually amused by how frequently the discussions turn toward securing one of the renowned crusade evangelists to conduct a crusade in their city. A frequent perception of the ultimate impact for God in the city is a citywide crusade. A report in one of our urban newspapers recently quoted a popular television evangelist as stating his intention to evangelize the entire world in his lifetime through his television preaching.

Dr. Ray Bakke of Northern Seminary in Chicago equates this mentality with that of our military command during the closing days of the Vietnam War. Greatly influenced by the demonstrations and negative press at home, and determining that we could not afford to keep losing so many of our men in the rice paddies of Southeast Asia, they devised a bombing strategy. Our B-52s on the island of Guam were assigned the mission of flying over enemy territory daily and bombing the enemy into submission.

This military strategy was about as effective in Vietnam as most crusades or media evangelistic efforts are in turning our cities toward God. George Peters of Dallas Theological Seminary has analyzed various crusade efforts in urban areas, and he states, "From the records and statistics available, there is no appreciable, immediate and measurable acceleration in church growth evident in most churches in the years following the campaigns."[3]

To effectively evangelize our nation's cities demands an approach more comprehensive than a "big guns" strategy. Massive ground troops must be mobilized who will live and die in the urban trenches for the sake of the gospel.

Evangelism, in its purest sense, is announcing the good news of the gospel of Jesus Christ. There is a unique essence about the story of Jesus. It is the pivotal truth for all human history. The gospel is not good advice which is only as credible as the advice-giver. The gospel of Jesus is good news of great joy, which is for everyone. It has been abundantly validated by his death on Calvary. Our ultimate challenge is to get the message out, and every medium available should be utilized in this commitment.

It must be realized in this connection, however, that the message of the gospel is far more than just propositional truths about Jesus Christ. The message, in fact, is Jesus himself. He is the Evangel, alive, indwelling his body, the church, seeking to be through us what he was in the body of flesh which died on the cross. It is at the point of our failures to incorporate this evangel within us that the hope of God's glory in the earth is tragically diminished. There can never be an effective strategy which sidesteps the place of the church in the city, or which superimposes technology or mass strategies in place of Christian soldiers who live totally for Christ and bear witness to his gospel in the urban relationships.

The message is too often confused and garbled in our cities by a multitude of urban realities which readily come to the mind of the secular hearer every time the gospel is proclaimed. The gospel will never clearly be understood by many urban residents unless the gospel is courageously applied to the urban and global realities which they face. Christians must declare that God's good news addresses the issues of race, class, exclusivity, poverty, hunger, housing, nationalism, violence, and a vast array of other concerns which crush real life from our world. The gospel of Jesus Christ is wholly radical because its aim is cosmic redemption, and anything short of that is a counterfeit faith. The Scriptures yield illuminating insight regarding the focus of our struggle in the cities. The apostle Paul said, "For our struggle is not against flesh and blood, but against the rulers, against the powers, against the world forces of this darkness, against the spiritual forces of wickedness in the heavenly places" (Eph. 6:12, NASB). When we commit ourselves to evangelization of urban America, we are challenging the strongholds of principalities and powers. Our enemy is the rulers of the darkness who are entrenched and boldly aggressive in urban America.

Of course, if our primary concern is on institutional statistical growth, then we can plant churches and do evangelism only in areas of rapid growth and economic vitality. Our growth charts will look good, and we can in large measure escape the heat of the battle. But if our mission is to proclaim the good news of the kingdom of God, we will have to look beyond simple statistical growth and set our sights on God's will being done in this earth as it is in heaven.

A black preacher in Roxbury, Massachusetts, testified that as long as he had lived on a farm in southeast Missouri he didn't have much trouble with Jesus' teaching about seeking first the kingdom of God and its righteousness and all your other needs would be taken care of. "Even in the bad years," he said, "there was enough food from the farm to keep from starving. But, when I moved to

Roxbury," he said, "I went through a time of thinking that Jesus just didn't know what he was talking about. Because you can starve to death in the city."[4]

If all of those in the city who know Christ will set their priorities on seeking the kingdom of God and his justice, many more folk who do not believe in Jesus will begin to hear and believe the gospel. Generally, Christians have not given nearly enough attention to building a platform from which to preach to urban people. Whatever platform we have had is shaky, indeed, from being bombed by years of racial and economic injustice, split apart by competitive strife among Christians, and consumed in the fires of pride, materialism, and greed. The Christian faith makes extraordinary claims about its sufficiency and power through Christ. But despite the resounding declarations from pulpits and evangelistic conferences across the land, the sophisticated, secular, and pluralized cities often render the faithful powerless and insufficient.

Cities call for a comprehensive and cooperative strategy. This strategy process will divide into at least three phases: dedication, discovery, and design.

New Dedication

Whether it is the individual believer, the local congregation, or the total community of faith, effective evangelization begins with our affirmation that only God is worthy of our time, our talents, all that we are, and all that we have influence over. Only a revolutionary encounter with the living God can equip today's church to face the formidable forces of darkness who wield such power in urban centers. This dedication must be both individual and corporate. Christians must call one another to account for singing songs of faith on Sunday while living the values of faithlessness during the week. Individual Christians must work and pray continually to bring their corporate bodies in which they participate into this same radical dedication.

Revolutionary fires sweep the earth, fanned by political forces which seek to change the balance of power. However, the volatile spark which ignites these world revolutions is the cry of every human being to be free to have dignity and to experience significance in life before death comes. The Scriptures speak of this human aspiration from beginning to end. God's gift of Jesus Christ was specifically offered as the ultimate answer to this need.

The urban evangelist must perceive the issues of the city in their global dimensions and dedicate themselves afresh to the radical gospel of the cross which alone provides the ultimate answers.

A Phase of Discovery

This is the phase of research and analysis. The discovery should focus on the total environment, demographics, attitudes, systems analysis, assessment of past history, and anticipation of future trends. The task of analyzing the context of the city should be seen as of extreme importance. The discovery phase should lead us to explore what God is already doing in the city through persons and structures who may or may not be in religious institutions. Some of our most valuable allies in sharing God's good news in the city may be the persons who do not profess faith in Jesus Christ but who are committed to building community and meeting human needs. Many mayors, housing commissioners, social service administrators, and law enforcement personnel are eager for Christian people to share their expertise and compassion in response to the human dilemmas with which they are faced. Each of these allies gives the Christian community an opportunity to witness to those in power concerning God's purpose for their individual lives, as well as for their exercise of responsibility and power in the city. These persons also open wide arenas of access to persons who have yet to respond in faith to Christ.

The discovery phase will help the Christians in the city find each other and unite their efforts for more effective impact. In an urban share group, a suburban pastor testified concerning how much this monthly time of sharing with other ministers in the city meant to him. He said:

> Were it not for the time with other ministers from all across the metropolitan area, my perspective on what God wants to do in this city would be severely distorted. I have some sense of what God is saying to me on my side of town, but it is absolutely essential to hear

what God is saying to you in other parts of this city in order that together we might learn more fully the strategy that God's people should implement.

The modern city comes at us with many shapes, systems, and changing patterns. Satan's strategies are complex and comprehensive. No one church or denomination can mount an effective offense against the principalities and powers by themselves. Jesus' prayer still echoes in the city streets, "I pray, Father, that they may all be one" (see John 17). Evangelism is our best hope for bringing a cooperative unity to Christ's fragmented body in the city. However, an evangelism which will unite us must be more than a one-dimensional, programmed gospel which speaks only of hope in eternity. If we can affirm the many facets of witness which the Holy Spirit has gifted the body to use and can incorporate our giftedness in the context of a holistic strategy, there is real hope for a broad spectrum of Christian participation. The discovery phase should help us to mobilize the great strength which Christian people do have in our cities if we will acknowledge how much we need each other.

The essential resource in the discovery process, however, is the mind of God. It is a sign of great hope today that many cities across America are developing broad-based coalitions of Christian leaders committed to each other and to the task of urban evangelization. In Pittsburgh, Chicago, Washington, D.C., Baltimore, and Atlanta, and possibly others I do not know about, there are Christian leaders discovering together the many variations on how God is using his body to lift up Jesus Christ in the urban context. The urban research task forces, mobilized by the Consultation on World Evangelization, brought together a body of data and developed a network of leadership which is enabling us to see for the first time the ways in which the Father is moving in our land. Another mobilizing force is the urban offensive groups generated through the Pittsburgh Leadership Foundation and the Pittsburgh Experiment. These new discoveries are being used of God to give his people new insights into urban strategy design which has tremendous possibilities for greater Christian impact on our cities in the years ahead.

Design

This phase in urban evangelization should include the following dimensions: preevangelism plans, direct evangelism projects and processes, evangelism conservation and discipleship, and continuing evaluation.

Preevangelism Plans

1. Train Christians in all aspects of gospel communication and ministry options. The kinds of training needed should be determined after there has been a real discovery of the giftedness of the body and an opportunity for the creativity of the Holy Spirit to generate options for witness and ministry that have not been traditionally considered. We must work continually at developing new training designs that equip the body for appropriate urban witness and ministry strategies.
2. Build a climate of affirmation for the witness of Christ by repenting of and removing the incongruence between the message of Christ and the life-style of the church. It should not take long in serious prayer and honest reflection to identify the practices, policies, and patterns of life which are significant hindrances to the impact of the gospel in a given city. There are things in the past which cannot be changed, but public repentance and reconciliation projects will speak of righteousness and justice and will open minds and hearts to receive the word of truth.
3. A communication and mobilization plan should call out the people and the financial resources needed to launch and implement the strategy. If the experiences of dedication, discovery, and designing have been entered into with a sincere dependency upon the Holy Spirit then we should conclude that what we are seeking to do is of ultimate importance and we should call out the members of the body to make the dream a reality.

Direct Evangelism Projects and Processes

Under this phase of the design will come a vast array of creative evangelistic options. If an evangelistic event or project is part of a well-planned, comprehensive strategy, one which gives attention to context, social, and cultural barriers, mind-set of the audience, and is undergirded by an affirmative witness to justice and righteousness, almost any means of communicating the gospel is likely to have impact. Direct evangelism design should maximize the natural relationships of Christians as the primary contact points for evangelism. Our traditional tendency has been to depend solely on programmed evangelism designs which oftentimes pull people away from their primary relationships. The cities of America cry out for reality and meaning in interpersonal relations. We must find a multiplicity of new options for calling people to witness in the context of their primary relationships. The next main heading in this chapter will deal with urban evangelism as practice and will provide some specific examples of Christians who are doing creative, direct evangelism in a variety of modes.

Evangelism Conservation and Discipleship

A primary part of the Great Commission is, "to baptize them and to teach them to obey all things I have instructed you." The local body of believers must be the place where conservation and spiritual growth is ensured.

In the cities a crucial part of the evangelizing process must be the planting of many new congregations in all types of communities where new believers can enter into a nurturing, loving fellowship which will enable them to grow up in Christ. Billy Graham wrote in the *Church Growth Bulletin:*

> It is an embarrassing fact that the churches in the United States and around the world which are geographically closest to the unevangelized people are often farthest away from them culturally and emotionally. This amazing new element smashed the illusion many Christians had that the world can be won if only the worldwide church will evangelize the people with whom it is normally in contact.[5]

It is my conviction that some of the greatest churches in America are yet to be planted in our nation's cities. Serious concern for evangelizing the cities demands a thoughtful and prayerful church planting strategy.

Continuing Evaluation

Though it is imperative to have a plan, it is equally imperative that every phase of the design be submitted to continuing evaluation. Our God is a dynamic, living Spirit who is redemptively responding to everyday circumstance. The design which is envisioned in prayer and research during the discovery phase will provide a vision and a vehicle for evangelization in the cities. We must acknowledge, however, that no human design is infallible, and God will probably give many new insights concerning his plan which will assist us along the way in correcting the course to achieve maximum impact.

Urban Evangelism as Practice

All of the efforts in praying, planning, and promoting will mean nothing at all in urban America unless the practice of Christians is evangelistic. There is never anything that can substitute for telling the good news of Jesus Christ. The following are reports on a number of ways persons in cities are telling the story of Jesus in the context of deeds, ministries, and lives of genuine Christlikeness.

Effective Evangelistic Urban Churches

Fairview Avenue Baptist Church on the lower east side of Detroit, Michigan, is one of the few institutions which have survived in this community of massive disintegration. Pastor Michael Nardin has led the church to view the community not as a place from which to escape, but a place in which to establish a stable reference point for hope and love. This church has had a remarkable capacity to readjust its focus for the changing needs of the community. They have majored on recreation and education programming for children and youth. They are viewed in the community as the place where the action is. A few years ago they established a community drop-in center away from the church property so the troubled teens and young adults from the community could be exposed to a Christian witness of genuine concern. They have been a primary resource for community action on virtually every community concern—housing, drug abuse, crime, education, hunger, health care, community services, and much more.

This has all been done in the context of a consistent communication of Jesus Christ as the only hope for their community. Even though this neighborhood has for ten years been among the most blighted areas in all of Detroit, this church is alive and stronger today than it has been in many years. The secret has been its continuing commitment to the vital *koinonia* of the body and a high level of trust and openness between the pastor and the people. They have sustained an evangelistic thrust because of their unshakable commitment to Jesus Christ and their untiring dedication to continually reshape the focus to meet the needs of people.

The old First Southern Baptist Church of Los Angeles was well on its way from decline to death twelve years ago when Tom Wolf was called as pastor. He challenged the church to stay in their transitional community and make at least a ten-year commitment to him as their leader. This challenge was taken, and immediately a number of things began to occur. One was that the perception by the church of its new residents in the community began to change from one of fear and apprehension to one of opportunity and kingdom growth. Another was that the name of the church was changed to The Church on Brady.

Today Pastor Wolf calls this thriving fellowship his "Hoab" congregation because it is made up of Hispanics, Orientals, Anglos, and blacks. Their concept of *oikos* or household evangelism has revolutionized this church and its evangelistic witness in the community. Each new convert is seen as an open door to an entire household or sphere of influence. The church moves with the new believer into his realm of influence to love and lead his family, friends, and acquaintances into the sphere of the church's love and ministry. Ultimately many of these receive Jesus Christ. The Church on Brady is projecting a new evangelistic thrust toward two high schools which serve their community. Strategies of cultivative witness will be directed toward students, faculty, and administration, as well as the homes of students who are responsive to this relational witness. These and many other holistic strategies have made The Church on Brady a dynamic, encouraging sign of kingdom life and hope in the city of Los Angeles.

LaSalle Street Church in Chicago is the bridge between Cabrinni Green, an all-black public housing community and Carl Sandburg Village, a high-rise luxury community of young professionals. Perhaps as well as any church in America, LaSalle Street has brought these two disparate worlds together in the fellowship of Christian commitment. Through their worship, they have purposefully incorporated the sounds and symbols of every tradition of their congregation. In their program design, they have mobilized the expertise of the young professionals to advocate justice and righteousness in Cabrinni Green. When the local public high school faced a budget crunch and the football program was going to be cut, the church launched a fund-raising effort to save the program. The result has been that a number of the athletes and other students now refer to LaSalle Street as "my church."

Bill Leslie, the pastor of this church for over twenty years, has also had a continuing witness to political leadership in the city of Chicago. Along with praying for and witnessing among these political leaders, he has won their confidence and thus has the credibility to speak the truth of God's Word to the powers in the city of Chicago.

Central Presbyterian Church in Atlanta is historic, sophisticated, and housed in a very impressive facility located across the street from the state capitol building. Each night this winter Central opened their building to hundreds of street people who had no place to sleep except out in the bitter cold. This act of Christlike compassion on the part of one church has pricked the conscience of many Christians in the city who are just now beginning to see the multitudes of people for whom there was no place in their city. Many of these poor, sick, and homeless pilgrims are for the first time beginning to feel and believe in the credibility of the Christian witness.

Numbers of other churches from across the metropolitan community have cooperated with Central in sending lay persons to stay through the night with these people from the streets, sharing with them their love and ministering among them in the name of

Jesus Christ. Along with what they have given, most of these church people also testify that they have learned a great deal more from these homeless pilgrims in the city. Central has led the way in addressing a crucial urban issue. May others follow in their steps.

In August 1980, Gene Bolin came to be pastor of a struggling mission church in the heart of Manhattan, New York. The mission had been initiated by the Greenwich Baptist Church of Greenwich, Connecticut, in 1976 but had faced considerable difficulty in securing pastoral leadership. Since 1980 this mission church has become one of the most exciting and growth-oriented churches in all of New York City. Their significant growth in the past two years has come because of the focus on friendship evangelism. The people have been trained and encouraged to share their faith along the relationship lines of their daily lives. Utilizing this life-style evangelistic design, they are becoming a dynamic, indigenous urban church, comprised of the multiplicity of people groups who call Manhattan home. In the church body, there are American black persons, French Haitians, Hispanics, Anglos, Israelis, Hungarians, students, actors, entertainers, business people, young people, old people, rich people, poor people.

The church employs various outreach efforts to witness and minister beyond themselves. Home Bible study groups are being established in strategic locations. Several from the church minister at Covenant House, which provides a ministry to children, teens, and young adults who are seeking to escape from the prostitution and pornography racket.

They also use telephone surveys to develop outreach contacts and engage in street witness dialogues in front of their building on West 72nd Street. Metro Baptist Church in the heart of Manhattan is making evangelism a practice and doing it effectively in our nation's largest city.

Temple of the Faith Baptist Church began in 1968 in a storefront building near West Side, Detroit, Michigan. The Reverend Rochelle Davis, his family, and a half a dozen other persons made up the congregation. Davis worked at the Chrysler assembly plant, went to school, and led the new congregation during the first five years of its rapid growth. By 1974 the church had moved three times because of inadequate space, then bought a building from a congregation which had merged with another church. The new building offered tremendous facilities for worship, training, and fellowship. The little church and its dynamic pastor took advantage of every opportunity. The first summer they planned a blitz on a large public housing community. Utilizing college student mission teams and Youth groups from other states, they conducted a Vacation Bible School, organized recreation activities, and established home Bible study fellowships. The children, teenagers, and their parents responded to these initiatives in phenomenal numbers. The church doubled its membership within the next year. Even though Temple of the Faith is predominantly a black congregation, members have reached out to everyone in their community without discrimination. They have continually had white members in the church body and have reached out to Jewish persons, Hispanics, and Asians.

The church is known for its community concerns, sponsoring and supporting a wide range of community ministries. There is a ministry with released prisoners and troubled youth. The church has also given birth to two mission churches which are now growing in the same pattern as Temple of the Faith. Under Davis's leadership, Temple of the Faith has been unashamedly evangelistic. They have lived the good news in compassionate deeds of mercy for all persons.

Coalitions in Cooperative Urban Evangelism

Voice of Calvary Ministries in Mendenhall and Jackson, Mississippi, is an evangelistic ministry based on a total community development model. The Reverend John Perkins founded Voice of Calvary Ministries twenty-one years ago when he returned to Mississippi after finding Jesus Christ as Savior and Lord while in California. He returned to his native community convinced that Jesus Christ could transform other lives in the radical way he had been changed. He also determined that if Christ could change individuals he could also redeem communities and bring people to a new confidence and competence in every aspect of their lives.

Voice of Calvary Ministries involves worshiping congregations as well as an ever-increasing number of community projects which reach people at the point of their needs. They have pioneered in the developing of thrift stores, health clinics, farms, training centers in evangelism, as well as economic development, the arts, and multitude of continuing education programs for youth. Voice of Calvary has demonstrated that the poor in Mississippi will respond and develop into great productive Christians when the good news of the whole gospel is consistently shared with them.

Riverside House in Miami, Florida, is an evangelistic and rehabilitation ministry to released prisoners. Directed by Cleveland Bell, a former prisoner and drug addict, Riverside House is supported by a broad base of churches and individuals from the Miami area. This evangelistic thrust targets one of the most crucial groups in any city. Bell has built this successful model on the premise that these men have fallen victim to the principalities and powers, the rulers of the darkness, and that their only hope for deliverance is in Jesus Christ. There is strong emphasis on Bible study, prayer, and the supportive Christian community who assist these men in practical ways toward rehabilitation.

Help the Children Project of Atlanta, Georgia, was born out of the trauma of the murdered children in that city. Sponsored by the Atlanta Christian Council and directed by Presbyterian minister the Reverend Bob Bevis, Help the Children organized clusters of congregations all across the metropolitan community to support and staff twenty-four ministries to the children in poverty neighborhoods. These ministries enrolled approximately three thousand children in Bible study, crafts, music, and recreation activities. Throughout the long weeks of agony because of the murders, Help the Children demonstrated the great potential of organized efforts focused on specific needs. The remarkable way in which congregations of many different religious groups came together on behalf of Atlanta's children is a parable of hope for the urban future. Help the Children continues in Atlanta.

The Shepherd's Restoration Project of the South Bronx, New York City, grew out of the massive destruction due to arson-related fires in this community. This coalition of eighty churches from many different denominations was developed in 1978 and has continued the steady pursuit of their dream: the restoration of hope, health, and community in the South Bronx. In cooperation with the New York City Housing Authority, the Shepherd's has undertaken the rehabilitation of housing in the communities served by the eighty congregations. The rehabilitation is being done largely with "sweat evangelism," volunteer labor from Baptist friends in the South and with tithed labor from the members of the churches.

As the buildings are rehabilitated, the Shepherd's institute a program of management and tenant training to build a level of competence and commitment to maintaining the property. As the volunteers work in the buildings, they share their Christian faith with inquisitive persons in the neighborhood. Bibles are made available to the new residents, and home Bible study groups are developed to share Christ's message in the restored buildings.

The Shepherd's Restoration Project is not primarily concerned with the rehabilitation of community buildings. Their real goal is the rehabilitation of the lives and the restoration of community in the South Bronx. They believe that sharing the whole gospel of Jesus Christ is the sure way to realize this goal.

Individual Urban Evangelists

Fred Roach is president of Centennial Homes in Dallas, Texas. Fred is a churchman who takes Christ with him in every facet of life. He travels a great deal. When he is away from home, he makes a practice of writing a letter each week to his son, witnessing to him about the values and strengths of the Christian life.

In his business relationships, Fred has made his faith in Christ the cornerstone of all he does. In training his executive staff in management of sales principles, he frequently uses Romans 12, emphasizing that they should not be conformed to the world's way of relating to one another and their customers but to acknowledge all that they do to be done in service to God. He speaks of the giftedness of people, especially those who know Christ, which can be used to accomplish God's purposes in all human relationships.

Fred has gained the respect of his business colleagues because his relationship to Christ is so natural, so attractive, and so obviously genuine. Fred Roach is continually involved in cultivative witness by praying for and befriending persons whom he has met who have not yet received Christ. Fred also is a street evangelist, a reaper of the harvest. As the spirit leads, he naturally and effectively encounters persons to talk with them about the great good news of Jesus Christ. Because of the authentic witness of Dallas businessman Fred Roach, there are persons all across the country who now live the Christ life.

Rosa Cruze has a dream. She believes the church and Christian business people can help address the massive problem of unemployment plaguing our urban environment. Through her initiatives, along with co-worker Marianne Thomas, the Christian Employment Transition Cooperative has been developed. The Christian employment transition cooperative is a cooperative of white and black congregations in metropolitan Atlanta who have united through the business persons in those churches to develop a job bank and to utilize strategically selected church facilities as the intake center for persons seeking employment. Rosa sees the cooperative as an instrument of touching persons at a point of high vulnerability in getting real assistance in securing jobs. Beyond that obvious objective is the pervasive concern in all the cooperative does to share Jesus Christ as the hope for all of life. Each client who is processed through the cooperative is counseled concerning life goals and directions. A witness concerning God's power and availability through faith in Jesus Christ is shared as the avenue through which the right job is secured. They pray with each person individually and continuously pray for all the clients that each one might find the abundant life which God desires. The desire of the cooperative is to expand the awareness of employers and business people in the church concerning their role in sharing Christ in the context of their business relationships.

Jim Queen is the pastor of Uptown Baptist Church in Chicago and is one of America's most effective urban evangelists. He is in no sense a typical pastor. He is not enclosed in structures and buildings where people have to search for him. He is a street evangelist, a community pastor who has unusual gifts in modeling Christ's love in telling the gospel story so that it receives a response. Whether Jim is preaching to his multiethnic congregation comprised of Cambodians, Laotians, Vietnamese, Hispanics, Anglos, and Indians or taking a group of street kids to a farm to gather donated corn for hungry people, he is continually calling people to faith in Jesus Christ.

Because of Jim's unusual athletic ability, he was used of God to direct the inner-city athletic mission for eight years during the 60s. Today there are young men all across Chicago who met Christ as a member of one of Coach Queen's teams.

Now, as pastor of Uptown Baptist Church, Jim still spends time with high school athletes, helping to coach the teams and conducting Bible studies for the students. During the summer, he organizes basketball leagues for the various athletes of the five north-side Chicago high schools, and through this league he continues his coaching, witnessing, discipling contact with young people.

With all his strength and athletic prowess, Jim is still the essence of Christlike meekness. In the comprehensive ministry of the church to children, Jim is at the center, caring in a tender way for the little ones whom Jesus loves. The church's caring witness with the poor and forgotten old people of Uptown Baptist Church is another arena which Jim Queen is highly visible. His life-style has both modeled and mobilized the varied ministries of evangelistic impact. Perhaps the greatest strength of Jim Queen is his capacity to inspire, mobilize, and equip others to move together with him in evangelizing the city.

Urban Evangelism as Priority

Dr. Ray Bakke argues that the period of church history from AD 500 to 1500 is known as the Dark Ages essentially because of the failure to develop an urban strategy. Drawing from Kenneth Scott Latourette's *History of Christianity,* Bakke suggests that in AD 500 the stronghold of Christianity was in the urban centers of North Africa. By AD 1500 the Moslems had virtually eradicated the Christian presence in the cities of North Africa, and the focus of Christianity was radically shifted from urban centers of North Africa to rural Europe. For one thousand years there was no real gain in the numerical strength of Christianity. There was simply a swapping of urban real estate for rural real estate.

The failures of the Church which brought on the Dark Ages were many, but Bakke suggests the following which reflect on their failure in the cities.

1. They refused to give the tribal people the Scriptures in their own language, except in Egypt.
2. The failure to indigenize their ministries—the bishops and priests were all appointed from Rome. Africans had little control over their own church.
3. They refused to deal with the race issue.
4. They refused to develop new approaches for the new urban realities.
5. The church leaders developed a desert theology rather than an urban theology. This led to an escapist, monastic life for the church.
6. Schisms. Churches after the persecutions of AD 250-258 were increasingly competitors of a wide range of issues. This led to increased energies for defensive apologetics, severing the nerve of mission and evangelism.[6]

A new period of "dark ages" for the Christian witness may be closing in on America and the world unless the cities become our top priority. The syndromes of urban avoidance, religious institutional power games, escapist theologies, and racial exclusivity all manifest themselves with disturbing frequency in American Christianity.

The urban challenge will not go away. It is, indeed, becoming more pervasive and complex with every passing day. The word of the Lord from the prophet Jeremiah is as apropos for our time as it was when the weeping prophet first delivered it. "Seek the shalom of the city where I have called you into exile, and pray to the Lord on its behalf for in its shalom you will find your own" (Jer. 29:7, *author's translation*).

As twentieth-century exiles in an alien urban land, our first priority must be to seek the peace of our cities or there will be no peace in America. We will have all eternity to celebrate our victories, but we may have only a few hours before the night falls to win them. Urban evangelization, priority 1.

Notes

1. Donald Baillie, *God Was in Christ* (New York: Scribners, 1948), p. 205 *f.*
2. Jacques Ellul, *The Meaning of the City* (Grand Rapids: Eerdmans, 1970), pp. 26-27.
3. Jim Peterson, *Evangelism as a Lifestyle* (Colorado Springs: Navigator Press, 1980), p. 30.
4. Shriver and Astrum, *Is There Hope for the City?* (Philadelphia: Westminster Press, 1977), p. 162.
5. "Billy Graham's New Vision," *Church Growth Bulletin* (November, 1972), p. 278.
6. Raymond Bakke, *Evangelization in an Urban World,* oral presentation to Forum on Urban Evangelism, Home Mission Board, Atlanta, Georgia, May, 1981.

8

Alternative Church Models for an Urban Society
Francis M. DuBose

Since mid century the church has undergone drastic changes in structure and style. Pressures have been both external and internal. Radical and sometimes revolutionary social changes, especially centered in the cities, have exerted pressures from without. The effort of the church to be the church in the midst of these changes has exerted pressures from within. This pressure-packed period has produced a variety of manifestations. A new religious rhetoric has emerged and with it a plethora of new slogans. Radical reactions have spawned new spiritual movements around the periphery of the institutional church, followed by new experiments of form and style within the traditional church itself. And there have been debates, dialogues, symposia, and seminars which have reflected on the impact of these movements and experiments. There has been action, and there has been reaction.

Now that the theological and methodological dust has somewhat settled from the rapid procession of this parade of church, parachurch, and antichurch manifestations—a variety of new trends seems discernible. From these trends, we are now able to observe emerging alternatives to traditional urban church form and life which promise a greater relevance to the emerging dynamic urban context.

Recent Pressures Demanding Alternative Models

The true nature of the church does not change. Therefore, its essential purpose remains constant: to incarnate in its corporate life and in the individual lives of its body members the love of God in Christ. The purpose of the church is to evangelize, teach, train, nurture, worship, minister, to be on mission in the world, and to bear prophetic witness to the gospel in all areas of life. How these functions are "contextualized," however, is not constant. The purpose of the church must be translated into viable and vital expressions which are meaningful to the lives of urban people and consonant with the realities of their daily experience. In other words, a church in an urban context must, indeed, be an urban church—though there may be a wide variety of shapes and styles within that urbanity.

The First Wave of Pressures

The first wave of changes which made a profound impact upon the traditional structures of social and church life emerged just after World War II and in the fifties. They made their full impact in the sixties. These changes were both social and religious in nature.

Radical Urban Social Change. Since mid century, there has been an acceleration of the rural-urban migration trend which began significantly in the earlier part of the century. The advent of the poor, tenant-farm population into the cities paralleled a vast suburban development. The "white flight" created both the transitional city neighborhoods and the new suburban communities, with church congregations reflecting this drastic urban social change. Unable to cope with change, literally thousands of American central city churches have moved, merged, or died in the last few decades.

At the same time, there has been a proliferation of suburban churches. Moreover, as white churches have moved from the inner city, black churches have moved in to take their places. Other minority church groups, such as the ethnic-language congregations, have also become prominent in the central cities. The inner city has always been the port of entry for the newly arriving immigrants.

With this vast suburbanization, urban areas have become so large as to meet each other, creating the strip, circular, and cluster city phenomenon. Metropolis has become megalopolis. The very size of the emerging urban giants, complicated by social variety, ideological pluralism, and economic disparity, has pitted city against suburb. This has created the city and anticity mentality which has been socially divisive and damaging in the new megalopolis.

With the emergence of the megalopolis have come the new megachurches of unprecedented size. Moreover, with the coming of the electronic age has come the electronic church, and with it a whole new concept of the church and a whole new set of problems. Just as each division of urban geography traditionally has created a form of church life indigenous to that geography (the downtown church, the inner-city church, and the city neighborhood church), so each new social aspect of modern urban expression has created some new form of church life which reflects that aspect (the suburban church and the church on the rural-urban fringe).

The Civil Rights Movement. Paralleling these drastic urban social changes have been a number of other social movements. One of the most significant has been the civil rights movement of the fifties and sixties. Essentially an urban phenomenon, this movement made such an impact upon the church that it led to a deep examination of the theological implications of "white flight." Also growing out of these influences was the creation of a large number of racially mixed congregations. Whites and blacks, now together in the megalopolis, have been cooperating with each other in unprecedented ways in the context of the changing city. The same development applies to relationships between whites and the ethnic-language groups.

The Rise of the Counterculture and the Jesus Movement

Another significant movement which developed in the fifties and sixties was a new counterculture development, primarily among the youth and young adults. It was a reaction in part to urban social alienation, but it was also a rebellion against the larger problems of the whole modern social system. The beatniks of the fifties and the hippies of the sixties were protesting against the social and spiritual emptiness of the modern, materialistic age. The urban centers most keenly witnessed the impact of this revolution. The Jesus movement which grew out of this counterculture revolt has had a strong impact on modern, urban church life.

Nostalgia and the Country Craze. Reactions to the pressures of change have expressed themselves both in the mechanism of rebellion and in the mechanism of escape. The mechanism of escape or retreat is manifested in the nostalgic "country craze" which is still sweeping the nation. This is best illustrated in the significant rise of country music, though it has expressed itself in other ways, from architecture to style of dress. A significant aspect of this phenomenon is that country has come to town. It is as electronic as everything else. The folk lyrics and melodies flow freely through the normal sophisticated channels of modern urban technology.

The Impact of Combined Pressures. Both the rebellious mood of the counterculture ideal and the nostalgic mood of the country ideal have helped to bring a greater simplicity and laxness to forms of worship, from the free churches to the liturgical traditions, including some of the Roman Catholic churches. These separately rooted and widely varying "ways" have met in the city, and urban technology has found a way to unite them. Many modern religious songs with a folk-rock flavor are sung regularly in virtually every church tradition, though not in all individual congregations and certainly not always on Sunday morning. They have provided the instrumentality and cadence for the lyrics which affirm a variety of urban themes, many of them reflecting the ideas of the civil rights movement and the ideals of the counterculture movement.

The Second Wave of Pressures

Now a second wave of influences has been sweeping over megalopolis. This has been in part a backlash from the more violent changes of the sixties. However, this wave also has implications reflecting a crucial world crisis which has strongly impacted life in the United States in recent years.

The New Refugees and Immigrants. The troubled world of the seventies has brought an avalanche of refugees to America: Vietnamese, Laotians, and Cambodians from Southeast Asia; Haitians and Cubans from the Caribbean; Salvadorans, Guatemalans, and other Hispanics from Central America. Add to this the continuing pattern of the nonregistered arriving from Mexico and other immigrants from Latin America and Asia, and the impact upon American life becomes obvious. A hundred years ago, 82 percent of immigrants to America were from Europe. Today three-fourths are from Asia and Latin America. This portends a far greater impact of ethnics upon church life than we have previously known. Already ethnic churches and ethnic departments of churches have significantly altered the pattern of American church life. This phenomenon has forced the churches not simply to be aware of the issues of the Third World but to be aware of the presence of the people from the Third World who are residing on their doorsteps.

The Conservative Backlash. The mid-late seventies have witnessed a new phenomenon, the movement away from the more progressive political and theological mood to a reactionary political conservatism and religious fundamentalism. Church people have felt threatened by the emerging pluralism, and strong reactions have come against the moral laxity in the country. This has expressed itself significantly in the growing number of Christian day schools among more conservative churches and in the virtual monopoly of the electronic media by the strong conservative and charismatic groups. A strong religiopolitical crusade spirit has captured many churches and church people.

A Wave of Spiritual Renewal. While this conservative reactionism continues to make its impact on church life, the more moderate contingent continues to be influenced by the theological and missiological implications of the great social issues of the day. Though there seem to be some recent losses in the arena of human rights, there are still deep concerns in these areas in the churches. There has been a growing concern for the problem of world hunger among the evangelical churches, resulting in large and unprecedented offerings for the poor and in a simple life-style movement. The concern to match justice and social action with evangelism and church growth is strong among the evangelical churches today.

The seventies have witnessed a continuing creative and heroic attempt to deal with issues which confronted the churches and society in the fifties and sixties. Many dying inner-city, transitional churches have received new life; a multitude of new compassionate ministries have emerged in the ghettos and transitional areas of the cities. One of the most conspicuous aspects of modern, urban church life is a whole new array of concerns and manifestations which go deeper than simply the style of music. One of these which is related not just to music but to the whole concept of worship is the idea of celebration. Of course, it has its roots in the recital theology and liturgy of both Old and New Testaments, but it seems to have been recovered today through the combined influence of the charismatic element delivered via the Jesus movement and the discovery by whites of the worship style of the black churches. Other influences, which have flowered in Baptist and other churches in the late seventies and early eighties and which have come in part through the Jesus movement, have been renewed emphases upon the spiritual gifts and upon the concept of shepherding. Though other groups have not carried this to the extreme form of the practice of "submission" typical of some charismatic groups, there has been a very strong development of a discipleship concept based on the "one-on-one" shepherding idea which the counterculture churches have strongly emphasized. This discipleship emphasis has reached almost movement proportions in the traditional evangelical churches, including Southern Baptist.

The Church Growth Movement. One of the most potent influences on modern church life which has made a significant impact particularly in the seventies has been the church growth movement. It was in part a reaction to the more liberal trends and the lack of a strong evangelistic and church growth emphasis in the preceding decades. Riding on the crest of the optimistic mood encouraged by the new spiritual movements around the world, this movement has produced an avalanche of books and has developed tools of church growth almost to the point of a science. As influential as it has been, however, it has not escaped criticism from both liberals and evangelicals. The evangelical critiques have come primarily at the level of what is perceived to be theological weaknesses and a pragmatic catering to a kind of Madison Avenue methodology expressed in instant successism.

The Rise of the Third-World Church. Most of the preceding observations have been based upon changes in the United States and the effect these changes have had upon church life. However, one of the most significant developments since mid century has been the new and impressive church congregational models which have emerged in the Third World: in Asia, Africa, and Latin America. For example, the super churches of today are in Asia and Latin America. No church in North America can compare in size, for example, to the Yoido Island Central Full Gospel Church in Seoul, Korea, organized in 1958 with now over 150,000 baptized members. And the requirements for baptism? Six months demonstrated faithfulness in: (1) tithing, (2) attendance at the weekly home cell Bible study groups, and (3) attendance each Sunday at celebration services of the mother church. The use of the satellite congregation has been developed most effectively by these Third-World megachurches in Korea and Latin America. The pattern of early morning, daily prayer meetings has grown out of vital church life in Korea and Africa. Also the pattern of weekday and beyond-the-church-walls ministries has developed strongly in Latin America and other Third-World areas, as well as in North America.

The Emerging Variety of Suggestive Models

It sometimes takes great wisdom to discern the difference between the passing fads and the innovations of an era which will leave permanent marks. In these days of revolutionary social change, there are so many uncertainties that permanent trends are difficult to determine. There are so many contingencies which could affect the structure and styles of the churches of the future: (1) fuel shortages, (2) gas prices, (3) automobile prices, (4) cost of real estate, (5) interest rates, (6) unemployment, (7) inflation, (8) recession, (9) depression, (10) revitalization of the central cities, (11) immigration policies, (12) refugee problems, (13) future technology, (14) nostalgia. Add to this the yet unborn political, social, economic, and spiritual realities and one becomes exceedingly hesitant about projecting into the future.

In response or in reaction to the dynamic factors of social change and the pressures they bring to bear on the urban scene, there do seem to be discernible patterns of urban church life which reflect three fundamental attitudes and identities which are institutionalized in the urban context: (1) *Reaction against urbanism* thrives on nostalgia and escapism and usually results in the "enclaving" and the "ghettoizing" of the church. Earlier storefront churches somewhat reflected this pattern. Churches today which start their own schools for racist reasons in order to escape the responsibility of integration or, for more noble reasons, to protect their children from ideological pluralism or from what they see as morally eroding influences of the public schools also fall in this pattern. These tend to create a society within a society and do not normally relate prophetically to the community at large.

(2) *Adaptation to urbanism* is the pattern of trying to structure church life in response to needs created by the daily pressure of urban life. The churches that major on fellowship and perhaps build around homogeneous units of support, though not always without some inroads into the community, basically follow this pattern.

(3) *Adoption of urbanism* is the pattern of church life effectively contextualized into the urban setting. The apostolic church is the classic example of this model. The heterogenous or multiethnic churches today, which relate vitally to both the public and the private needs of urban families and which speak prophetically to the social issues of the day and function as redemptive change agents in society, follow this pattern. They have established themselves on the wavelength of the urban mind-set in the public sphere and, at the same time, have been sensitive to the needs of urban persons in the private sphere. Thus they balance mass communication with small group involvement (primarily through house church units).

Changing Patterns

Changing patterns of urban life have strongly altered traditional roles of various congregational types. Indeed, a whole new series of church types has emerged, calling for new categories and reclassifications of congregational types. Recent trends in larger church life have strong implications for the pattern of local church form and life.

New Patterns of Change. The recent trends which have

strongly affected the pattern of contemporary urban church congregational life are numerous. They may be summarized as follows: (1) the blending of traditional congregational types, (2) the regionalization of the congregation, (3) the tendency to shift church leadership in the megalopolis away from the downtown toward the suburbs, (4) the continuing central city exodus of churches and the deepening crisis of the transitional churches, (5) yet paradoxically the more recent trend of the renewal of city churches, (6) the explosion of the suburban churches, (7) the multiplication of ethnic churches, (8) the growing prominence of the black church, (9) the recovery of the house church.[1]

New Church Types. The traditional classic urban church congregational types are: (1) the cathedral, (2) downtown old first, (3) the uptown church, (4) the people's church, (5) the university church, (6) the neighborhood church, (7) the storefront church, (8) the black church, (9) the ethnic-language church, (10) the suburban church. However, this traditional classification has not been sufficient to encompass the complex new congregational developments in the post World War II era of the megalopolis.

New categories have become necessary: (1) the regional church, (2) the church on the rural-urban fringe, (3) the mega-church, (4) the base-satellite church, (5) the federated church (of house churches), (6) the multicongregational church, (7) the multiethnic church (church of the nations), (8) the exurban and rurban church, (9) the ecumenical church (parish), (10) the relocated church in a redeveloped area, (11) the special purpose church, (12) the life-style church, (13) the rural church in an urban world.[2]

In fact, Lyle Schaller believes there has been such a revolution in urban congregation life as to call for a totally new way of classifying churches. He types them as follows: (1) the church on the plateau (four levels of numerical growth), (2) the ex-neighborhood church, (3) the ex-rural church, (4) the teenage church, (5) the youth to maturity church, (6) the *Saturday-Evening-Post* church (the church in transition).[3]

Recent Trends in Local Churches. Lyle Schaller, one of the most astute observers of changes in the contemporary church, has noted the following as recent trends which promise to have a significant effect on the pattern of future local church life: (1) the congregational use of local cable television, (2) the controversial trend of the proliferation of Christian day schools, (3) the erosion of denominational loyalty, (4) young adult as well as children's ministries, (5) the decline of the traditional Sunday School but the growing strength of weekday Bible study groups in homes, on campuses, and in business settings, (6) earlier Sunday morning services because of national sports activities, (7) the tendency of church educational curriculum to be structured less around traditional categories of age, gender, and marital status and more around levels of spiritual development, reflecting the different stages of the faith development of the adult.[4]

The Emerging Definitive Patterns

Even though it is difficult to be positive about just how definitive certain trends are, there are today a series of patterns so clear and consistent, so universal and crosscultural, as to make one reasonably positive about their relevance, at least for the foreseeable future.

Seven-Day-Week Church Life. The last few decades have witnessed a return to the apostolic pattern: "and daily in the temple, and in every house, they ceased not to teach and preach Jesus Christ" (Acts 5:42). Changing patterns of work, changing needs of people, the fast pace of life, the emergency nature of needs, changing patterns of study and play, and other factors have caused the churches to continue their ministries beyond Sundays throughout the week. This is more than the midweek prayer service, the weekend Youth activities, or the use of the church facilities for traditional groups, such as the meeting of Scout troops. Almost every conceivable type of social service is being provided in churches all over the world in weekday programs: feeding programs, tutoring, language classes, seniors' ministries, clinics, counseling, legal aid, job placement, food pantries, clothing, sewing classes, craft instruction, auto mechanics, music lessons, drama groups, literacy education, friendship groups, and referral services. This is in addition to the expanded weekday educational curriculum of the churches and the weekday worship services.

These weekday activities in many cases are expanded beyond the church walls, in homes and in various locations within the community. Also the daily pattern of early morning prayer common in the churches of Korea and Africa fit into this pattern.

Ministry Beyond the Church Walls. Related to the weekday programs is the growing tendency for the churches to augment (sometimes significantly) their ministries with a witness beyond the walls. Worship services may be held on Sundays in numerous places other than the central church facility. For example, the Nineteenth Avenue Baptist Church of San Francisco sponsors a "Believer's Chapel" on Sunday evening at the University of San Francisco. Churches have outreach preaching points and home meetings of numerous varieties. Churches sponsor coffee houses, halfway houses, street theater, prayer breakfasts, and luncheon and dinner fellowships at restaurants and hotels. They run book stores and thrift shops and are even forming business companies to provide employment for their members and jobless community members and to support evangelistic and ministry outreach programs.

Churches cooperate with community organizations and often furnish office and conference space and provide creative leadership for such groups. Sam Simpson, pastor of the Bronx Baptist Church, has led his congregation in joining with others in literally helping to rebuild sections of the Bronx through creative approaches to new housing projects for the community. Allen Temple Baptist Church of Oakland, among its many community-related involvements, combines street evangelism in the ghetto (winning drug kings to Christ) with political activity to elect morally responsible leadership in the city. The Assembly of God Church in Calcutta, India, feeds over ten thousand hungry people a day in the destitute areas of the city. A leading Uniting Church congregation in Sydney, Australia, has developed a network of social programs over the city which rivals any social service program in all of Australia. The First Baptist Church of Niteroi, Brazil, among its sixty-five preaching points, has a service at the boat station where Niteroi residents ferry to and from the city of Rio de Janeiro. More than five thousand persons have professed Christ in these services in the last two decades.[5] Baptists and other evangelicals in Bangkok, Thailand, have launched a house church revolution in one of the most difficult areas for the gospel outside of the Muslim world. The Baptists alone have identified one thousand neighborhoods which they have begun to "climatize" with the view of starting house churches. In the city of Manila, there has been the creation of hundreds of small Bible study groups organized and conducted by Christian laymen from the business community.[6]

Multipurpose Use of Church Facilities

Another clear pattern has been the development of multipurpose functions for the use of church buildings. Older churches have remodeled or have simply adapted. Recent church construction, such as that of the West Memorial Baptist Church of Houston, has been designed totally to accommodate this concept. Every room in the facility has a multiple purpose. This movement has developed in order to provide for the growing number of innovations in education, worship, and related creative approaches to church life and also to accommodate the expanding number of special programs of Christian social ministries.

Another use has been to provide space for constructive parachurch groups, student groups, interfaith fellowships, community organizations, and nonpartisan civic groups. In some cases, the church may participate in the causes of these groups but not always. Sometimes the churches have rented space to such groups and to other groups, such as special education schools, night community college classes, and so forth. This has given churches high visibility in the communities, provided unprecedented open doors to hearts and homes, and has given a vital witness of redemptive caring in the community.

Another significant development in this regard has been the sharing of church facilities with sister ethnic-language congregations. In some cases these may not be of the same denomination, but in most cases they are. In some instances, traditional Anglo churches have sponsored such language congregations, even several of them. For example, the Nineteenth Avenue Baptist Church in San Francisco presently sponsors or relates closely to Cantonese, Vietnamese, Japanese, Korean, and Arabic groups, which all share the same general facility. In some cases the congregations in time move out into their own facility such as the Mandarin congregation of the Nineteenth Avenue Baptist Church has recently done. An interesting recent phenomenon which has developed among Southern Baptists in San Francisco has been the sponsorship of another group by an ethnic congregation itself. Grace Chinese Church, for example, has sponsored a new English congregation and the American Indian Church has sponsored a new Hispanic work. In both cases, both congregations share the same facilities.

Increasing Lay Involvements

Most of the exciting spiritual developments which have brought new life and vitality to the churches have related to lay renewal. There has been a new lay witness emphasis in the churches. The renewed emphasis on the gifts of the Spirit affirms that there is an essential and vital place for every Christian in the body of Christ. The new discipleship emphasis has strong lay overtones. The weekday ministries in and outside the traditional church facility and the many beyond-the-walls church activities would have been impossible without massive lay involvement. The most phenomenal marshaling of lay leadership by a single church in modern times, if not in the entire history of Christianity, has been accomplished by the Yoido Island Central Church of Seoul. Some 15,000 lay shepherds lead as many home Bible study groups every week.

An Emerging Model: The Church of the Nations

A new model now being developed out of the growing phenomenon of multiethnicity, and through careful theological reflection, is the concept of the "Church of the Nations." It is an effort to affirm both creation and redemption—on the one hand to acknowledge, respect, and affirm cultural differences, but on the other hand to unite the body of Christ in one larger church family. A practical dimension focuses upon the problem of the traditional loss to Christianity and the church of the second generation children of ethnic parents in language churches where English was not permitted to be used for these children. This was at the time when they were using English in every other area of life: school, play, social activities, and most other out-of-the-home peer relationships.

No doubt numerous patterns will emerge within this larger model, but some of the basic structures now emerging are as follows: (1) There will be weekly worship services in each of the several languages with a common service ideally once a week but at least once a month. The services will be translated but not just from English to other languages (ideally with a rotation system in which each language is equally affirmed). This of course will be difficult if there are more than two or three languages involved. Also, various unique features of the respective groups will be affirmed, such as the use of traditional musical instruments. The various groups can learn simple versions of songs in the other languages.

(2) There will be language classes for Sunday School and other educational functions where they are needed. (3) There will be common classes in English for all English-speaking children, youth, and adults. (4) There will be common gatherings of all groups for the Lord's Supper, baptism, prayer meetings, fellowships, special functions, outreach training, and other functions. (5) There will be a common budget, with a strong stewardship teaching program and allocations made on the basis of *needs.* (6) There will be a common calendar with each group respecting every other group in terms of special calendaring needs unique to each specific group. (7) Each group will affirm every other group in terms of felt needs to preserve positive cultural values, especially those with strong moral implications, under the common lordship of Christ. Classes and activities which affirm a group's language, culture, and traditional ethnic values will be accepted and respected so long as they do not become divisive and disruptive to the fellowship of the larger life of the church family.

(8) The development of an equitable pastoral staff concept and practice admittedly is one of the most difficult barriers in the way of

perfecting this model. Most of this is due to nonbiblical "hang-ups" about pastoral leadership. Ideally, there should be complete equality of designation (title, etc.), salary (with a scale based on *need*, number of children, etc.), administrative position and authority, freedom within each ethnic group, office space and design (allowing for personal differences), and all other functions. Serious efforts should be made to understand the significance of the cultural impact of the symbols related to this arrangement, to be as certain as possible that each group is equally affirmed.

Two models of leadership are presently envisioned, both without the "senior pastor" concept: (a) a democratic board of pastors with a rotating leader and (b) an administrative leader who would be the business manager, coordinating the various groups and the common and unique functions of the church community. He would not be a "professional pastor type"—the pastoral leader would be the pastor of each group. There would also be one diaconate for the whole church body, variously organized to help the pastors meet the needs of all the people. An ethnic advisory committee from each group should be created to work with their pastor for the purpose of keeping the unique needs of each respective group before the larger community. (This model would no doubt work with the "senior pastor" concept despite the built-in dangers of paternalism, as, indeed, it is working with varying degrees of effectiveness in varying patterns of this emerging model.)

(9) There should be a common business meeting based upon democratic principles, with each group being free to meet as a group to make decisions for recommendation to the general body. (10) There should be every effort to design the most flexible structures possible to ensure an openness to the Holy Spirit's leadership in all things. (11) The spirit of the church should be thoroughly missionary with outreach basic to its structural concern. The pattern expected is that this church would give birth to churches after the same model. The above is the model toward which the Nineteenth Avenue Baptist Church of San Francisco is moving.

Creative House Groups: The Most Promising Model

Despite the revolutionary changes of the past decades, much of the past is still with us. These patterns of the past are so deeply engrained, they are not likely to disappear in the foreseeable future despite the changes transpiring all around them. Traditional patterns likely to remain are: the Sunday morning worship service, Sunday School, the traditional church building, pastor-centered church life, the business model of the church, white churches, ethnic churches, black churches, and so on. Even the more recent patterns of church life, which have already become somewhat institutionalized, give strong indication of persisting at least into the foreseeable future. Some of these are the storefront church, the white enclave congregation in transitional multiracial community, the "show-biz" electronic church, and so forth. Despite all the theological treatises and denominational strategies, some churches will continue not to learn and will continue to move, to merge, or to die.

The Wave of the Future

Churches which respond to the wave of the future, however, will find exciting new prospects of healthy growth and an expanding witness on the horizon of the emerging megalopolis. Church house groups (commonly referred to by some as house churches) are a part of that wave of the future. The reason for this is the fact that they are a contextualized Christian form of the small-group phenomenon which has risen in recent decades out of necessity, as a response to the intensification of urbanism in the emerging megalopolis. A small group revolution has been sweeping across the world in recent decades. They range from the more secular, psychologically-oriented "touch" groups to the extremely religious groups, some of which are cultic and occultic in nature. Somewhere in between is a multitude of wholesome groups. As a balance to the public sphere of mass relations in an urban society, the small groups are a reflection of the private sphere of personal relations of the primary groups in an urban society. The primary group with its small group expressions is normative in the urban way of life, but such expressions in recent decades have exploded into an almost infinite variety of manifestations in the wake of the most extensive and intensive urban revolution in history.[7]

Allen Toffler in *The Third Wave* makes an impressive case for what he calls "the Electronic Cottage." He marshals considerable evidence in support of the return of "the Home-Centered Society" through home-based electronic industries. Of course, he does not see the "third wave" reinstating the traditional nuclear family of working father, housewife mother, and two children. Rather he sees a kind of postmodern "Electronic *Expanded* Family." This is not the classical "extended" family but a third-wave "expanded" family.[8] Some of the house churches with their business-related operations are a kind of prototype of one possible style of this "expanded family," though in some cases without the electronic implications.

House groups, therefore, must be seen as indigenous forms of the church in the emerging technological society of megalopolis. They are kin to other "relational" types of church life and witness, such as the coffee house. Other manifestations of this larger family-oriented, strongly "relational" movement are the Christian Ashrams of India and other parts of the world,[9] and the more politically conditioned "basic communities," particularly of Latin America.[10] The concept of *oikos,* household evangelism, a growing emphasis today, is also a reflection of this larger movement.

The Significance of House Groups

Besides representing the wave of the future, the house group commends itself for an impressive variety of reasons: (1) it constitutes a natural setting for the household of faith; (2) it is a New Testament method;[11] (3) it is indigenous to urban life; (4) it is the most economical of all ways to begin new work and to nurture Christian life; (5) it is a flexible method, dynamic and adaptable; (6) it appeals to people who are uncomfortable with the formal church setting; (7) it appeals to all classes, types, and ages; (8) it works in all areas of the world; (9) it lends itself to an amazing variety of styles;[12] (10) it is possible when no other form of Christian meeting is possible. The strength of Christianity in the Soviet Union and in China today is due to the underground house churches that have persisted over the years and decades. It is estimated today that besides the official "Three Selves," formally recognized church of China, there are several million people who meet each week in house churches.

Nothing has impressed me more than house meetings I have attended in various parts of the world in recent years. One Sunday morning I attended a house church service in a multistoried, lower income, housing project in Madrid, Spain. The next week I conducted a Bible study for a house group meeting in Paris, France, in the spacious home of an American diplomat, attended by English-speaking embassy people from various parts of the world. I have been in home meetings with middle-class apartment dwellers in Kobe, Japan, and with students in a high-rise apartment complex in Caracas, Venezuela, where a young student couple invites fellow intellectuals to study the Bible every week. I have attended Bible study house groups in San Salvador, El Salvador; in Buenos Aires, Argentina; in Lusaka, Zambia; in Bangkok, Thailand. I have visited a house church service in the home of a wealthy rice farmer in Kediri, Indonesia and house church services in the homes of untouchables and low castes near Bangalore, India. I have spoken at house church services in Calcutta and Singapore. I have attended many house church groups in the San Francisco Bay area, some very informal, others as formal as any formal service in a traditional church sanctuary.

Answers to Objections to House Groups

Because we have drifted so far from the New Testament pattern of house churches and because we are so captive of the "edifice complex," it is understandable that there are always objections to house groups. Let us speak to the more obvious ones. (1) Is there enough space? is an often-heard complaint. The simple answer to this is to develop a style commensurate with the space available. In fact, the amount of space is one of the key factors in developing the type of group possible in various homes. Obviously, groups can do more in spacious homes. However, humble homes are often more conducive to other more desirable dimensions of church life. (2) What do you do with the children? In

Third-World countries, this is not the problem it is in North Atlantic countries where children are not as integral to all functions of life. Where it is a problem, groups convinced of the value of home meetings have found ways to handle it.

(3) The neighbors will complain. The fact of the matter is, neighbors normally do not complain about well-ordered home meetings of their neighbors. However, house groups should be very sensitive to this matter and be certain this is not a problem. (4) People want to go to a church that looks like a church. Fine, encourage them to do just that. Others who are uncomfortable in formal church settings will be attracted to home meetings. (5) Religious proselyters and cranks will take over. It is true that this can happen but not if groups are prepared for it and deal with it firmly and immediately, though always tactfully and compassionately. (6) Home meetings interfere with home life. This can happen, but those sponsoring house groups should be especially sensitive to this matter. Only families which truly want to host these groups and only those secure enough to handle them should be allowed to host them. In most cases, it works the other way around—house meetings help to stabilize the families where they meet.

(7) It won't work here. I have never been to any part of the world (North, Central, and South America; the Near and Far East, and Africa) where I did not hear this complaint; and I have never been anywhere in the world where house groups did not work. While someone, usually from an older church group, is saying it won't work, others, usually from a younger church group, are making it work at that very place or in the general area.

Types of House Groups

Most of the Christian house groups can be classified under three major categories based upon their relationship to other churches or church group. (1) *The autonomous house churches* are independent church congregations which differ only from other churches at the point of where they meet and in the style of congregational life inherent in that reality. They are not structurally dependent on another church congregation. They may or may not be denominational. If they are, they relate to the denomination just as any other autonomous church would.

(2) *The federated house congregations* are semi-independent church groups which function separately, with their own pastors (though they may be bivocational or students) and have their own meetings and activities, yet relate in a definitive way to one or more similar groups. Part of the identity of such groups is a sense of relationship or even belonging to these other house groups. They usually meet together from time to time for various functions (celebration, prayer, Bible study, training, fellowship, social life, recreation), yet it is not centralized.

(3) *The satellite home fellowships* are centralized. They are a satellite expression of a larger centralized church body to which they are structurally related. They may differ in number, size, distance from the mother body, content, and style; but they all have in common a dependence on and accountability to the central base church of which they are an integral part.

Types of Households Which Sponsor House Groups

House groups are hosted by a variety of household types.

(1) *The nuclear family households* may host an autonomous house church, usually being a vital part of the church group and probably providing major leadership if not the pastoral position itself. They may also host a federated house congregation or relate to it. However, they are more likely to host a home fellowship which is a satellite of a mother church.

(2) *The extended family households* are more likely to exist in Africa or Asia or among minorities in the North Atlantic world. They are just as apt to host one form of these house groups as another. The family structure, however, makes it a good beginning base for an autonomous or federated house group. In some cases, there are enough extended family members to constitute a full congregation in its own right, though they all may not necessarily reside under the same roof.

(3) *Singles households* are ideal for an autonomous or federated house group, though they may host home fellowships as satellites. It is not uncommon in the San Francisco Bay area for a

group of singles to rent or even buy a large house and turn it into a combination residence and house church. It is an excellent strategy.

(4) *The communal family households* are also ideal for the autonomous and federated house churches, though they may also function as satellite fellowships. This model may be an expanded family, which begins as a nuclear or even extended family base. There may be one or more father-mother families or childless couples, with singles completing the "family." It may be made up only of singles. However, it is well organized, with a strong sense of responsibility and accountability. There is a family orientation with a sharing structure based upon the communal concept.

These communal households have also been called "Christian Houses." They are organized usually around one of three basic concepts: (a) There is the "residence" model, primarily designed as a place where persons "reside," but as a family unit. (b) There is the "leadership" model, primarily designed as a fellowship of potential church leaders organized under a father-teacher figure for the purpose of training in some type of Christian service, especially for a defined period of time (a family-oriented dormitory and informal theological seminary). (c) There is the "ministry" model designed primarily as an outreach fellowship where mature Christians "take in" new Christians or non-Christians who have special ministry needs (the halfway house concept, but much more on the order of a ministering expanded family). All of these models have been developed to varying degrees, especially in the San Francisco Bay area. One "leadership" training model is illustrated by the Christian Ashram of India.

The Style and Content of House Groups

The genius of house groups is that they are suited for an almost unlimited potential in outreach ministries. They also exist in an almost unlimited variety of expressions. This enables them to meet the many and varied needs of people in the urban context. Some of the more immediate functions are as follows: (1) a full church function of worship, teaching, training, fellowship, stewardship, outreach; (2) Bible study for evangelism and/or nurturing; (3)

teaching, various instruction with a wide curriculum potential; (4) training in sensitivity skills; (5) prayer festivals; (6) fellowship for believers and friendship evangelism; (7) friendship groups built around avocational or specialized interest; (8) craft training; (9) art groups; (10) language study; (11) Christian social ministries; (12) halfway houses; (13) workers meetings; (14) various alternative community models of the church, etc.

The Base-Satellite: An Ideal Model

Although no church congregational model is perfect, the most ideal for the emerging megalopolis seems to be some variety of the base-satellite. The greatest enemy it has to overcome is that problem common to all people and groups: the tendency to be selfish. It has the following advantages: (1) It addresses in one model the need for both massive and small group structures of communication which are integral to urban life. (2) It, therefore, offers the needed balance of impact (through the base) and penetration (through the home meeting). (3) It offers in one model the advantages of the larger church (base) and the smaller church (satellite). (4) It satisfies both the more traditional desires through the base and the more innovative desires through the satellite. (5) Its mobile and more secular expressions help effectively to con-textualize the church structures, making them more indigenous to urban life and form.

(6) It is a universal model which has been effectively demon-strated in all major parts of the world. (7) It is proving to be the model of the most impressively growing churches. (8) It is workable in any ethnic, denominational, or national tradition. (9) It has encouraging potential for balanced growth. (10) It has excellent potential for the development of new units which can become new churches. (11) It has potential for the application of sound theologi-cal and methodological insight to the meaning and significance of recent changes and emerging trends in church life and form.

Summary Principles on Beginning House Groups

In conclusion, it seems appropriate to list the vital principles necessary for getting seriously into the business of developing house groups. They are: (1) Make house groups a priority in denominational and church strategy. (2) Decide on the types needed. (3) Secure the sponsoring homes (inspire nuclear and extended families to host house groups and inspire the development of an "expanded" family concept and strategy for house groups. (4) Select and train the leaders. (5) Provide ongoing training (constant in-service training) for potential new groups. (6) Decide on the curriculum. (7) Decide on a design for the meetings. (8) Anticipate and be prepared to deal with all potential problems. (9) Be especially prepared to deal with cranks and proselyters. (10) Build in a sense of responsibility. (11) Affirm the importance of this ministry. (12) Free people to give priority to this calling. (13) Plan well for all details relating to the house group meetings. (14) Plan well for all other matters related to the house groups (advertising, visitation, invitations, transportation, equipment, etc.). (15) Be flexible. (16) Build in a strong sense of reliance upon the Holy Spirit and prayer. (17) Study effective models.

Whatever the structure, style, and content, house groups should maintain a strong missionary sense. The one element all effective groups have in common is the *koinonia*, but New Testament *koinonia* is not a closed society—it is always open-ended. The church as family must always be open and must always be reaching out. It is in this outward reach that the greatest maturing comes. We mature in mission. "That which we have seen and heard declare we unto you, that you may have fellowship with us: and truly our fellowship is with the Father, and with his Son Jesus Christ" (1 John 1:3). This is not the only message, but it is one of the most meaningful words the church must say to the world. This is not the only way, but it is one of the most meaningful ways the church can express itself to an urban world. The world of the urban future belongs to the churches which will be able, under the Holy Spirit's leadership, to create the most effective home meetings in which to multiply themselves and therefore to multiply their ministries in the world.

Notes

1. Francis M. DuBose, *How Churches Grow in an Urban World* (Nashville: Broadman Press, 1978), pp. 76-83.

2. Ibid., pp. 84-93.

3. Schaller, pp. 39-148.

4. Schaller, "Seven Trends That Are Shaping Church Life," *Presbyterian Survey* (Jan., 1982), pp. 18-20.

5. Mike Crewell, "Brazilian Church Sets Dizzying Place," *World Mission Journal* (March, 1982), pp. 6-7.

6. *The Thailand Report on Large Cities*, report of the Consultation on World Evangelization Mini-Consultation on Reaching Large Cities, Pattaya, Thailand, June 16-27, 1980. (Wheaton, Ill.: Lausanne Committee for World Evangelization, 1980). pp. 12-15.

7. DuBose, pp. 82-83; See also Donald R. Allen, *Barefoot in the Church: Sensing the Authentic Through the House Church* (Richmond: John Knox Press, 1972); Philip and Phoebe Anderson, *The House Church* (Nashville: Abingdon Press, 1975).

8. Alvin Toffler, *The Third Wave* (New York: William Morrow and Company, Inc., 1980), pp. 210-242.

9. P. O. Phillips, "The Place of Ashrams in the Life of the Church in India," *International Review of Missions* (Vol. XXXV, 1946), p. 265.

10. Jose Marins, "Basic Ecclesial Communities," Workshop Paper IV, *International Association for Mission Study*, Bangalore, India, January 4-10, 1982, pp. IV, 6-16.

11. DuBose, pp. 54-57.

12. Ibid., p. 163.

9

Urban Strategy Through Cooperative Efforts
Don E. Hammer, Jere Allen, and George W. Bullard, Jr.

If we are going to have a meaningful mission strategy to win our nation to Christ, it will be developed through the association. . . . Our total denomination must work together in reaching our land for Christ. We will do it, not independently of each other, but cooperatively working through the most basic unit we have beyond the local church—the association.[1]

This pronouncement by one denominational executive reflects the views of many others who also recognize that the cooperative grouping of churches within a city is essential if effective Christian witness is to be realized.

"Our strategy is to address the city as it is," said a Chicago mission leader. "If [we] are going to win the Chicago area [seven million population], we are going to have to be ethnic." In response to this challenge, one religious group, the Chicago Metropolitan Baptist Association, has set a 1985 new-work goal of adding 100 new churches and missions to its 1980 total of 112 churches; 75 percent of the goal is for non-Anglo congregations—25 percent black, 25 percent Hispanic; and 25 percent other ethnic groups.[2]

Such striking statements from church leaders underline the crucial role of the local association or conferences in mission strategy planning for the cities. This chapter will build upon these significant statements and will discuss several basic definitions, the need for urban strategy, some primary strategy assumptions, and one denominational process model for developing urban strategies for large cities.

Some Basic Definitions

The following terms merit some clarification: strategy and association. *Strategy* is generally understood to refer to a careful plan or method for advancing toward a goal—a framework or master plan, upon which more specific decisions and actions and action plans are based. Strategy involves decisions by persons and groups with the ability and authority to judge what is important to their locale.

Defining a denominational organizational expression such as *the association* is a little more difficult. Denominations have different structures; but in the Baptist tradition, the term *association* refers to a local organization. To Methodists, the district would be a similar unit of organization. Loyd Corder, a Southern Baptist mission leader, has popularized the definition: "The association is essentially churches in fellowship on mission in their setting."[3] Whatever the term used, we are referring to a local organization composed of individual churches of one denomination which, hopefully, share common interests and purposes.

The challenge of this chapter is for mission leaders in metropolitan areas to devise deliberate, responsible, God-directed strategy. Supporting or subsidizing a series of worthwhile projects of witness and ministry does not necessarily constitute a strategy—no matter how much money is invested or how worthwhile the projects. Increasingly, mission leaders will be faced with the negative forces of urbanism that burn like a forest fire roaring out of control. Sometimes, they opt to employ small hand extinguishers against the flames in their immediate surroundings, while major blazes continue to roar out of control in the larger region. The result—they win a minor battle in the neighborhood, but lose the larger battles in the city.

A comprehensive metropolitan strategy would first devise a plan to attack the major fire, restrain it, and then turn to the smaller blazes. For mission strategists, this would entail:

1. Devising a statement of purpose,
2. Doing a comprehensive analysis of the demographics, social systems, local churches, other religious groups and organizational structure;
3. Determining basic goals, calendaring, and resourcing action plans (tactics).

Such an approach, for example, is precisely what the Chicago

Metropolitan Baptist Association has devised to enable its churches to address Chicago "as it is." However, all local mission leaders are well aware that strategy is an enabler, not an end in itself. Mission is not completed when urban strategy has been developed, any more than a house is completed when the blueprint has been drawn. Effective urban strategy in metropolitan areas requires flexibility and open-endedness that allows for both internal and external changes.

Need for Urban Strategy

Why is there a need to plan a comprehensive urban strategy through the metropolitan association or conference? Why not be content to plan at the local church level? Several responses are in order.

First, no one local church has the expertise, resources, or base for developing a strategy that can deal with the massiveness of an entire metropolitan area.

The United States is not what it used to be. Times have changed! Urban people are bombarded by waves of urbanism. Dynamic urban life impacts every church and every association or judicatory. Multiple stimuli affect mission leaders.

This accelerated expression of multiple stimuli is due to a number of factors:
1) more and more people live in (and around) large metropolitan areas,
2) the growing complexity of urban life due to increasing heterogeneity and pluralism,
3) the increasing massiveness of urban institutions,
4) the increased amount of stimuli from a more prominent and complicated communications system,
5) the rapidly increased mobility of accelerated systems of transportation,
6) the new and threatening ideas and ideologies which bombard the average person,
7) the general growing complexity of every walk of life due to the networking of the above factors.[4]

In Chicago, for example, what can one congregation do alone

in a city of seven million people? Can a congregation cope in an area where ethnicity is the order of the day? Or where the largest population of Poles reside outside of Warsaw? Or where more than one million Hispanics reside? Or where blacks comprise almost one-third of the city's population?[5] The task of developing a mission strategy is staggering for all the congregations of any given denomination, but absolutely overwhelming if such a strategy has to be implemented out of one congregation's resources.

The mission field of cities like Chicago is receiving particular emphasis in many denominations. Though denominations like Southern Baptists have a love/hate relationship with the cities, they are still determined to do something about the people who reside in these massive megalopolitan areas. Whether they are talking about uptown Chicago, East Los Angeles, or Liberty City in Miami, mission strategists are concerned about places where the gospel of Jesus Christ needs to have an impact. They are becoming convinced that the local association or conference is the best base for building mission strategy to penetrate the target groups of people in these larger metropolitan areas.

Second, the very complexity of the social systems in the large cities requires a joint strategy approach at the local level. In every city, there are basic social systems which influence lives and, as such, impact judicatories and congregations. The social systems are political, economic, housing, education, health care and support, law enforcement, transportation, and others. The interaction of these social systems—when coupled with the history of the area, age of communities, physical environment, amount and rate of change, as well as the general attitude of the people toward such change—combine to overshadow single congregations and require churches to band together so they can be on mission throughout their cities. These social systems provide the dynamic interchanges that touch people through their various networks. How these social systems are valued varies from region to region and has an overwhelming impact on the culture of an area.

However, we must also note the effect of the media in linking these systems together. Overexposure in any of the social elements can color the distinctiveness in any locale. Thus, these systems affect people, and people under the proper leadership can affect systems. Effective church and denominational leaders—who want to be on the cutting edge as change agents—can utilize such media exposure to bring about urban change.[6]

Third, there is need for a comprehensive evangelism strategy for an entire metropolitan area. Many denominations remain overwhelmingly rural and small town in outlook and outreach. Only about 10 percent of Southern Baptist churches are in areas of more than one million people (megalopolitan areas). Twelve to 15 percent of Southern Baptist church members are in areas of more than one million people. Such figures are in stark contrast to the basic population statistics of America. Nationally in areas of more than one million people, there reside approximately ninety-three million persons, or 41 percent of the country's population. In metropolitan areas of less than one million lives 35 percent of the country's population, leaving less than 25 percent of the population living in nonmetropolitan areas.[7] Despite the efforts Southern Baptists have made in some of the great cities of America during the past twenty-five years, and the growth they have been able to achieve, these statistics point out their relative inability to penetrate larger urban centers for Christ.

Many churches in the city guard their independence very jealously, and such an attitude causes some churches to resist working together in evangelistic activities. But no church can evangelize a total city, in spite of the fact that many churches genuinely believe they can reach a much larger area than their church neighborhood. The fact remains that most churches are neighborhood in type and tend to minister and reach out to one major socioeconomic group or one region of the city. In this process, many segments of the population can be missed with the gospel of Christ.

Mainline Protestants have generally been upwardly mobile in social status and tend to reach white, middle-class, family-centered, often rural-oriented people. Because of this, they miss certain segments of the population who are inherent parts of the central city's mix—poor, migrants, blacks, and ethnics. Moreover, the deterioration of some central cities and transitional neighborhoods has resulted in many church members, and many of their churches, retreating to the suburbs. This results in the Christian witness being weakened in too many communities just at the time the population is on the increase. However, the newcomers—who are causing the population to increase—are not of the same socioeconomic and/or racial makeup as the church membership. The challenge before these churches is to devise new approaches for evangelistic outreach and ministry.

Again, to use the Chicago model, Southern Baptist work has been organized for less than twenty-five years in that great city. The strength in the churches has been drawn largely from displaced Southerners who moved to Chicago to find work. Today, although the rural mentality is still prevalent in some churches, the association is developing a greater appreciation for cultural and racial plurality. In fact, the Chicago Association's executive director warns, "The association must learn to embrace diversity, rather than shrink from language, cultural and social differences—if it is to be a viable force in pluralistic Chicago."[8]

He understands his role to lead associational leaders to develop a comprehensive evangelism strategy that enables the churches to reach out to all the people in the city. To accomplish this, he must work with his mission leaders to devise a methodology for beginning new missions, churches, and preaching points in all areas of Chicago.

Fourth, there is a need to develop an urban strategy for redistributing the resources of funds and personnel for the areas of greatest need. The greatest resources tend to be in the affluent, suburban churches, while the greatest needs are in depressed areas of the cities. Many churches will give funds to mission centers but will not give of themselves to social and spiritual needs of the disadvantaged in the central city. Insulated by suburban prosperity, some congregations are unaware of the great needs of people in transitional communities and of the imminent changes occurring in their own neighborhoods. Such mission problems/

challenges cannot be met as effectively by the solitary congregation. And they cannot be solved by some outside agency. The interrelated nature of the metropolitan area demands that churches, metropolitan judicatories, and denominational agencies cooperate more closely in their mission efforts to plan for reaching all people in the city.

The redistribution of resources is equally important in the beginning of new work, both in purchasing new church-building sites and in providing financial assistance, whether it is in new suburban areas or older neighborhood areas. An overall metropolitan church extension plan is the most logical base for recommending a location for new work.

For the reasons mentioned above, Southern Baptists, for example, have emphasized for the 1980s that it is the role of the association to be a mission strategy base for developing goals, action plans, and resources, as well as for recruiting volunteers to meet the challenge of the cities.[9]

Some Strategy Assumptions

In order to understand what is necessary to develop an adequate urban strategy for metropolitan areas, these strategy assumptions/ideas should be noted:

1. No single urban strategy is applicable to every metropolitan area. What works in Chicago or New York will not necessarily be the best planning model for Houston or Atlanta. If several associations/conferences are involved in a large metropolitan region, separate planning actions probably will need to be taken for each one.

2. The "best urban strategy" generally will come from the grassroots leaders. That is the value of a planning model that is locally-owned, custom-made, and open-ended. However, for such strategy to be successful, it will be based upon solid teamwork among church, association, state, and national leaders. Obviously, local churches begin the teamwork relationship at the judicatory level, but such teamwork moves to the state or synod level and then to national agencies through

their domestic mission agencies and church program agencies, so that proper resourcing can be made available for action plans. It is true that local churches can do many things; but a cluster of churches on mission at the local level can have the manpower, resources, and insights to pull together the best possible mission strategy to meet the most pressing needs of the entire region.

3. An adequate urban strategy will deal with the context of the metropolitan area. Basic demographic questions should be asked. Some are: What are the characteristics of the people who live in the area? Can the metropolitan area be described as a pluralistic community? What is the attitude of local mission leaders toward their context? Can they be motivated to respond? These and similar questions must be dealt with in the light of the unique context.[10]

4. An effective urban strategy must be one that takes into account the entire city, not just the central city, suburbs, or fringe areas. For example, in New York City, it is the whole "apple"—five boroughs—which is the concern of mission strategists, not just the Manhattan core.

5. Urban strategy must consider what other denominations are doing in the city.[11] It is important that denominations find ways in which their mission action plans can be interfaced in order to come to grips with the many needs that are present within a given metropolitan area. Some are finding that a federated approach—where denominations work together, based upon their own particular concerns and strengths—is a viable course of action. One national agency which facilitates this type of strategy is the Joint Strategy and Action Committee (JSAC), a coalition of sixteen national mission agencies. This group has developed a federated missions strategy for metropolitan Baltimore, Maryland, as a pilot project.

6. Urban strategy must involve identifying various target groups of people. A shotgun approach will not be as effective as specific target group evangelism strategies. A comprehensive urban strategy in evangelism will be a series of strategies

which attempt to address the different needs and interests that various segments of the population possess. Such strategies will take into account the needs that exist in age, ethnicity, culture, and language of the various people in the city.

For many mainline denominations, this will also entail coming to grips with the whiteness of churches. The cities of America have large nonwhite populations and these groups have their own mission leaders who have much to offer those who seek to minister within the city. In fact, a mission strategy for a major metropolitan area that does not include a strategy with blacks and ethnics will be inadequate and almost no strategy at all.

7. An adequate urban strategy must be prophetic. It is obvious that "business as usual" will not get Christ's work completed in the city. There must be something unique and even radical about successful metropolitan strategies. It is as if the strategy, to be successful, will have to be "other than the norm."

8. Urban strategy must involve kingdom dreams. The question must be asked: What is the kingdom dream for this metropolitan area? Though this question is difficult to answer, church and associational leaders must grapple with and answer it.[12]

9. Urban mission strategy must consider the calling, recruitment, training, placement, and tenure of ministers. Many ministers are needed who will accept pastorates in the central city, carry out adequate mission strategies, and be committed to longer tenures. This adds stability to congregations and mission strength to community structures.

10. Urban strategy must also consider the structure of the metropolitan association. Should there be multiple associations covering the same metropolitan area? Should there be one large organization which covers the entire megalopolitan area? Or, should there be several organizations in a large megalopolitan area, banding together in some federated or

correlated committee to carry out an overarching urban strategy for the area? These questions should be resolved based on the unique context of a given city.

A Denominational Process Model for Megalopolitan Strategy

Based upon the needs for an urban strategy and its assumptions, it seems appropriate to examine one denomination's megalopolitan strategy model. The Home Mission Board of the Southern Baptist Convention has developed—under the leadership of the Metropolitan Missions Department—a special process which is designed to develop an urban strategy for megalopolitan associations: "Mega Focus Cities."[13]

Mega is a term used by the Home Mission Board to designate a population area of more than one million people. The word *focus* designates the concentration of as many resources as possible into a given megalopolitan area. This mega area will be, for a period of time, the center of concentration, activity, and planning in implementing an adequate urban strategy. The emphasis is intended to surface the larger metropolitan areas for a special planning focus and resourcing. Southern Baptists, who comprise the largest Protestant denomination in the nation, have made little more than a token appearance in many of the United States' largest metropolitan areas. Yet, they realize any viable future strategy for growth and ministry must place an emphasis upon these megalopolitan areas.

How do we reach the cities? is the question that weighs heavily on Southern Baptists' minds. The Home Mission Board suggests a follow-up on a previous, three-year emphasis focusing upon key cities with a broader-based Mega Focus Cities emphasis, which would utilize resources at national, state, and local levels to build a basic foundation for witness and ministry in the country's major urban areas.

The Mega Focus Cities emphasis concentrates on five megalopolitan areas per year, beginning in 1983 and going through 1991. The purpose of Mega Focus Cities is to assist the churches, individually and cooperatively, in a given megalopolitan area through their metropolitan association strategy planning process.[14] The genius of the process resides in taking a metropolitan strategy planning process and coupling it with a Strategy Resource Team from the program areas of the Home Mission Board. In addition, the process calls for brokering the strategy needs and action plans with other agencies of the Southern Baptist Convention in an attempt to make this a denomination-wide strategy.

Building upon these initial learnings, Mega Focus Cities is an attempt to emphasize and develop a three-year process for the whole megalopolitan area. The first year involves negotiations and contracting with the state conventions and metropolitan associations, as well as orientating metropolitan church leaders to the dynamics of an adequate mission strategy. The second year requires developing an associational strategy plan, along with the proper resources from state and national agencies. The third year, or the focus year, is for beginning the strategy implementation.

It is anticipated that the strategy that has been developed will be placed into full implementation the year after the focus year by local, state, and national agencies which are pertinent to that urban strategy.

While special emphasis will be given to the association in the central city, each association in the region will be aided by state and national agencies in developing a separate federated strategy approach. Again, Mega Focus Cities seeks to honor the strategy assumptions put forth in this chapter by having a team approach of national, state, and local agencies working through the association and local churches. Each level of denominational structure will be an equal partner, and major actions will be by consensus.

One of the key elements in the process is that ultimately the Mega Focus Cities emphasis calls for total teamwork of Southern Baptist agencies. For the first time in history, Southern Baptist Convention agency leaders are talking with state and local leaders about a concentrated planning approach to reach the large megalopolitan areas.

Thus, recognizing this vast potential, Southern Baptists are excited about projecting this planning umbrella. In its initial pilot year of 1982, Mega Focus Cities had a limited planning design for two cities—New York City and Miami. The 1983 cities are Baltimore, Buffalo, Detroit, Louisville, and San Francisco. As can be seen by the listing, some areas that are reaching toward the one million mark are included in this strategy effort. Louisville is one of these. The 1984 focus cities will be Saint Louis, Fort Lauderdale/ West Palm Beach, Cleveland, New Orleans, and Los Angeles.

By 1991, plans are to have a strategy umbrella for the fifty largest megalopolitan areas in the United States. To do this would mean serious planning efforts would be in place for over 46 percent of the entire nation's population! Mega Focus Cities will not only concentrate on the ethnically diverse cities of the Frost Belt, where Southern Baptists have been concentrating new efforts for the past twenty-five years, but will also concentrate on the boom and the change in the cities of the Sun Belt. This latter emphasis is mandated by the lack of sufficient growth in these cities among Southern Baptist work.

Conclusion

The resources are scarce in comparison to the opportunities! Increasingly, as inflation eats away at mission dollars, denominational agencies should place major dollars where most of the people are located. Since the people are in the largest cities, this is where resources should be concentrated. The Mega Focus City approach represents a move in this direction by one denomination, but greater efforts are needed throughout the Christian community if the cities are to be reached.

All denominations must realize the diversity of the cities. Mission leaders must regain their ability to dream the dreams that altered the destinies of men and changed the shape of their world. It is true that people in the churches will seldom rise higher than their leaders. So the mantle falls on those leaders in the churches and denominations of today—inadequate and imperfect though they may be—to be willing to be God's instruments, and to dream the possible dreams for America's cities.

Notes

1. William G. Tanner, "The Association and Bold Mission Thrust," *Review and Expositor,* LXXVII (Spring, 1980), p. 159.

2. David Wilkinson, *Urban Heartbeat* (Atlanta: Home Mission Board, 1982), p. 144.

3. Loyd Corder, "Churches in Fellowship on Mission in Their Setting," (Atlanta: Home Mission Board, 1976).

4. Francis DuBose, "Our Urban Future, Issues and Implications for the Church" (Paper delivered at Urban Training Cooperative Breakfast, St. Louis, Missouri, June 11, 1979), p. 1.

5. Wilkinson, p. 144.

6. Don Hammer, "The Context of Associationalism," *Associational Bulletin,* October/ November, 1981, p. 5-6; also see Jere Allen, *Social Systems Study Guide* (Atlanta: Home Mission Board, 1981).

7. George Bullard, Jr., "An Introduction to Focus Cities," Unpublished paper, Home Mission Board, Atlanta, Georgia 1982.

8. Wilkinson, p. 145.

9. Southern Baptist mission leaders convened a national conference, "Missions in Context," at Ridgecrest, North Carolina, September, 1981 to introduce/train local associational leaders in 1980 census interpretation and new strategy planning instruments.

10. Robert E. Wiley, *Population Study Guide* (Atlanta: Home Mission Board, 1981).

11. _____, *Other Religious Groups Study Guide* (Atlanta: Home Mission Board, 1981).

12. George Bullard, Jr., "Developing Mission Strategies for Larger Metropolitan Areas," Unpublished article developed for *Church Administration,* (Nashville, Sunday School Board, n.d.).

13. Bullard, "An Introduction to Focus Cities."

14. For complete details on Association Strategy Planning process, see James Hamblen, *Associational Strategy Planning: Designing Your Association's Mission Strategy* (Atlanta: Home Mission Board, 1981).

10

Reaching America's Cities
G. Willis Bennett, C. Kirk Hadaway, and Larry L. Rose

Both American cities and the churches within them have been in trouble in recent years. Not too long ago serious questions were even raised regarding whether the churches would be able to survive urbanization. It seems clear enough that urbanization is here to stay, and the worn-out inner cores of many cities are at last showing signs of redevelopment and revitalization. The revitalization of church work in the cities during the past decade provides reassurance of the churches' survival as well. Perhaps persons of faith never stopped believing that the church, founded and blessed by Christ, has a quality of permanence. That it is here to stay is not the question. However, the form and structure the church takes is another matter, as is the issue of what it means to be the people of God in an urban setting. In other words, how should the church be shaped and how should it function in order to effectively reach America's cities with the gospel?

Affirming Our Purpose

Previous chapters have pointed out that the church is to function as the people of God on mission with Christ in the world and always to witness to God's glory. It is the goal of the church to bring all humankind into reconciliation with God and each other. This calls for knowledge, insight, commitment, and serious effort.

Our purpose within the church must be geared to those efforts that will go on building up the believers in the Lord and providing them with the necessary training to reach out in witness and ministry. Internally, within the family of God, this means providing for worship, education, and fellowship so individuals can grow into the kind of persons God wants them to be. Externally, these

158

committed disciples of the Lord are then to reach out in witness and ministry, individually and collectively, in order to impact the urban communities in which they live. Ministers and other professional church and denominational leaders have the responsibility to try to make provision for Christian growth within the congregations and to lead out in structuring and managing the congregational witness to the communities.

Sometimes these purposes will cause us to reconsider the quality of our witness in light of a particular situation. We may be pressed to more serious research and analysis of the urban context in which the ministry is to be pursued. We may discover that that ministry may take a variety of forms. It is likely to be both traditional and experimental. It may be within the walls of a church, but it is certain to move beyond. The ministry to persons and structures will extend into the neighborhoods in places of residence, work, and play. It will go beyond the neighborhoods, with attention to entire cities, seeking to influence those structures that serve humanity and those that dehumanize and oppress it.

The church today needs to place emphasis upon worship and celebration, upon education and discipleship training, upon evangelism and Christian social service, and upon addressing issues of social justice both by word and action. To do any one of these to the neglect of the others is to fail in a significant aspect of the church's purpose. Therefore, we would reaffirm the whole.

Accepting the Urban Setting

The work of the church has always seemed more difficult in the urban setting. No matter how lofty our goals or optimistic our attitudes, ministry in the urban church always brings us back down to earth. A pastor who has always led churches to substantial growth is called to a once prestigious downtown or inner-city church and expects growth to occur there as well. He tries all his well-worn techniques; he adopts denominational programs or strategies from famous "church growth" specialists. But nothing works. His church continues its slow decline. In despair, many of our urban ministers have questioned their calls and their abilities as God's servants. Many have even left the ministry to others who may have answers that they obviously lack.

It is little wonder that many pastors and other church professionals avoid the city church in favor of more "productive" situations in the sprawling suburbs of America. We are so used to city churches having problems that we think they are inevitable. So why take the risk? Obviously there are, indeed, risks involved in urban ministry, but they must be taken. The cities of America are in place and are with us now and into the distant future. They will not go away nor can we expect such a massive decentralization of America's population that they can be ignored.

As Paul Geisel notes, "The American city is in trouble, and when the city is in trouble, the country is in trouble." We are an urban nation and can no longer afford to neglect our cities and allow them to decay, as has happened to so many since World War II. Areas like the South Bronx of New York City do not occur naturally; we create them by our housing, taxation, and banking policies. Slowly, cities across America are starting to realize that they have qualities which are worth saving. Often the change can begin with a symbolic revitalization, such as the Renaissance Center in Detroit or the Inner Harbor in Baltimore. All at once the city is no longer viewed as a bad joke. Residents no longer bad-mouth their city from suburban retreats. They rediscover its identity and history and begin to defend it when outsiders are critical.

This symbolic change in attitude is very important because it marks a reversal in our national ambivalence toward the large city. We come to realize that they do not have to be "grim and worn out" but instead can be vital and exciting places to live and work. Our churches must become part of this revitalization process and learn to be at home in the cities—not by flowing back in with the gentry, but by becoming indigenous in whatever neighborhood they are located. We must be willing to stay in the city, but not merely to "stick it out" because it would be cowardly to leave or simply to maintain an outdated worship service for an aging remnant. There must be a *positive* reason for staying. Our churches should become true neighborhood churches again and act as positive forces in the future of the local community.

It is essential for the urban church to begin to understand its community setting and also the tendency of neighborhood congregations to become *captive* to demographic and cultural forces in American society. Such an awareness is the first step in overcoming forces which tend to control the church and limit its ability to minister. After all, it is not the environment alone which causes churches to grow or decline; it is how the structure of the church and its ministries match or do not match the setting which produces the strong relationship. Without this awareness, churches tend to blame their pastors; pastors either blame themselves or their congregations. Perhaps some churches do have "incurable diseases" as Peter Wagner suggests, but most do not and all "sick" churches have a fairly long period in which to act before their illness becomes too severe.

In summary, urbanization is a fact of life in the United States. At long last our large cities show signs of regaining positive identities which were lost years ago. Our churches and our membership must come to see the city as home, as an exciting place to live, work, and minister.

Understanding the Church and Its Urban Setting

Too often, as church leaders, urban missionaries, or denominational officials, we plan for urban outreach and ministry "by the seat of our pants." We think we know our church or community when we really do not and act on the basis of a very limited understanding. Even worse, at times we do not plan at all but spend our days "putting out fires" while our churches drift along without direction or meaningful goals.

Throughout this book the need has been stressed for an awareness of the city in its many facets, an understanding of the churches, their structures, strengths, weaknesses, and then action on the basis of some rationally determined strategy. All of these are desperately needed in the urban setting, and especially essential is the process by which leaders come to understand their churches and their context. Needs are all around us, and so we tend to jump from an awareness of a need to action without truly understanding the more general context of the problem. In all situations of church planning, research is essential in order to give some factual basis for the development of goals and objectives.

Without research into the structure and needs of a community it is very easy to mistake vocal needs for the more salient situations which should be addressed. The squeaky wheel gets the grease. An entire ministry can be based on responding to the most expedient needs, but such a ministry will have very little direction to it. Few goals will be accomplished other than the goals of the persons pushing for help. Similarly, it is difficult to know what action to take on the basis of pressing ministry needs unless research is done to pinpoint exactly where the ministry should be organized and how it should be carried out.

New churches, for instance, should only be included as a priority in an overall strategy for a city if there is a pressing need. Some type of new church development is called for in most cities, but research into population trends and the present location and constituencies of churches already present is the only way such a need can be determined. Once it is decided to start new work, further research is called for to determine what type of church should be started and where it should be located. Where are the fastest growing neighborhoods? Where is the largest concentration of an underevangelized ethnic group located? Is some other component of the population being missed, such as deaf persons, blue-collar workers, blacks, or singles? Questions like these are answered through research as part of the larger planning process.

We have seen in earlier chapters just how powerful is the impact of the local community context on the church. The findings of chapter 6, which dealt with the impact of the setting on churches in Memphis, came from a quite simple research project which could be conducted in any city. The goal of such research is to gain an overview of the health of churches in an entire urban area and to pinpoint areas and churches with particular problems or strengths. Additional information is needed on a wide variety of factors, but not so much as to overwhelm the planner or planning committee. The purpose, after all, in collecting data is to gain a better understanding of the situation. Once the data is collected, it must then be used to inform planning. New insights will be gained and they must be acted upon as part of an overall strategy plan for the city (or for the local church as a part of an overall urban strategy).

Planning: An Essential

Innovation and *flexibility* will be the key words for the church in America in the 1980s and 1990s. Willingness to be innovative and flexible in response to a changing society and its needs will determine the viability of the church. If churches and denominations are unwilling to do serious study of their contexts and to continually develop ways that the gospel can be more effectively shared, they will face great stress and loss. Any serious study of history will show that unwillingness to change usually means extinction. Methodology and theology are not the same. Many times methodology becomes so entrenched that we confuse our methods with our theology, thus thinking our methods are sacred and cannot be changed.

However, for those churches and denominations which are willing to commit themselves to the serious study and strategy development which has been suggested by this book, the 1980s and 1990s will be exciting and productive times for sharing the gospel.

How should planning for the church or judicatory be conducted? There are many possible designs, and the following six steps are only an illustration of how the process could possibly flow.

First, the planning group must take into account the context/ environment. To be effective we must learn our neighborhood/ region/city. This demands accurate data, interviews with leaders of organizations that serve the area, and the personal commitment to be students of the area. Shortcuts will result in spurious data that will then lead to faulty planning.

Second, the planning group must do a self-study of what they are doing and what they have done over at least the last five years. This honest reflection will help the planning group to be more aware of their real strengths and weaknesses in light of the area in which they are seeking to minister.

Third, the planning group must be representative of their constituents. There must be a serious effort to involve key leaders in the planning process if the strategy is to be effective. The church and association must feel that it is their strategy. Outside "experts" can be helpful; but unless the local group feels that the strategy is theirs, it will have little hope of working.

Fourth, resources must be committed in line with the needs. This speaks not only to the local planning group but also to the denomination of which the group is a part. We can no longer hope to reach the masses in the urban areas if our financial and personnel resources are primarily committed outside these urban areas.

Fifth, the planning group must *work* at their strategy. Reaching the cities of America will not be easy. It will take tremendous sacrifice. Jesus said, "If any man will come after me, let him deny himself, and take up his cross and follow me" (Matt. 16:24). One of our problems today may be that we want results for which we are not willing to pay the price.

Sixth, the planning group must, on a regular basis, evaluate their strategies and make needed changes when it becomes clear that certain tactics are not meeting needs as intended or if changes in the area show that they are no longer needed. Evaluation has been a glaring weakness of the church, but if we are going to be serious about reaching the cities of America we must include in our strategies an honest evaluation process.

New forms of church life will likely emerge out of this kind of serious approach to planning. New models, innovative programs, and new avenues of ministry will need to be designed by and for the churches in our cities.

We do not know what the future will bring, but one thing is certain: it will be different from the present and will create new needs for ministry and evangelism. As Orrin Morris has said in his chapter dealing with our urban future, "Since the future does not exist, it must be invented." We will create it through our own efforts. Therefore, what we *plan* and *implement* today will shape the church in the city tomorrow. If we fail to act, however, as William Pinson suggests, "Perhaps God will raise up another people to do what we would not do. Or he may let the inevitable wages of our sin be paid. . . ."

The Validation of Ministry to Metropolis

Throughout this book has been woven an emphasis upon an interdisciplinary approach to urban ministry. It should be evident that the various authors are committed to taking into account the social context of ministry. A particular city presents its own unique set of problems and opportunities with which organized religion must cope. Sociological approaches, with special emphasis on demographics, must be explored with care. Factual data, whatever its source, must provide the basis for planning.

Analysis is also needed. All the factual data which can be obtained will be of little value unless an authentic interpretation of that data is made. What does a city do to people? How are their lives affected by the multiple pressures and influences to which they are exposed? When people are caught up in their frustrations and fears, their loneliness and despair, their temptations and doubts, their achievements and joys, their opportunities and challenges, how are they likely to respond? And is there a word from the Lord for each of the circumstances?

The theory of this book is that ultimately ministry to metropolis is validated by faithfulness to theology, but a theology which does not hold itself aloof from the other disciplines which serve to inform it. When these various authors have spoken of cultural captivity of churches, problems related to church growth, opportunities for evangelism, new church models for ministry, or the biblical mandate, it has become quite clear that each is in search of an authentic theology which will enable the church to remain faithful to its purpose and mission.

Every human concern is a concern of God. The church that wants to reach America's cities must concern itself with these human concerns. Christians cannot be good interpreters of the gospel of Jesus Christ or good representatives of the concerns of the Father if they remain indifferent to any of the human problems with which humanity struggles in the urban context. It is not enough that the Word be proclaimed; it must become flesh and be demonstrated. It is not enough that prayers be offered from holy altars; they must motivate the faithful to join God in action.

Theology is for the marketplace as well as the sanctuary.

Human life, no where more than in the city, is lived in a social context. Persons interact with each other daily, and what they do to, for, and with each other reveals the character of their beings. They have the chance to give evidence to the Christian belief that they belong to each other. Even before the day of Christ, and not necessarily in a religious context, Aristotle said, "Men came together in cities in order to live; they remain together in order to live the good life." The good life is possible when human beings are willing to commit themselves to solidarity, to preservation, to true humanity and fulfillment, and to God's truth that all of life is precious and worth redeeming.

This work of the church will enable it to seek out the lost and let them know that God is in the city. He speaks the words of love, encouragement, hope, and salvation. The church wants to proclaim the words and enflesh them. We rejoice when the "one lost sheep" is found. The masses in the cities present to the church an unending task.

The task is made more complex when we recognize that our valid theology presses us to commit ourselves to a still larger and related task. It is the task of trying to fashion an environment wherein redeemed human beings can then live their lives in a context that contributes to their own growth toward the potentiality God wishes for every person. The circumstances of such a social context are not confined to beautiful church sanctuaries and facilities or even extensive programs and activities within those facilities. The lives of human beings are influenced by all with which they come in contact. Our theology and our Christian mission force us, therefore, to be concerned about housing, health care, education, employment, and all the agencies and institutions that help to create the urban life-style of any person.

Forever the message of the church will remain the same: "Jesus is Lord." The way we proclaim it must show that we believe that Christ is Lord of all relationships and organizations that help fashion the destiny of persons. He is present in the city and it is for us to join him and help make him visible.

No single denomination can do all things for all people, but each denomination can do some things. Let us, therefore, begin with that part of the work of the kingdom which God has called us and plan a holistic strategy, implement our plans, evaluate them, and depend on the Father for the results.

Contributors

Jere Allen is associate director, Metropolitan Missions Department, Home Mission Board of the Southern Baptist Convention, Atlanta, Georgia.

G. Willis Bennett is William Walker Brookes Professor of Church and Community, The Southern Baptist Theological Seminary, Louisville, Kentucky.

George W. Bullard, Jr., is national consultant, MEGA Associations, Metropolitan Missions Department, Home Mission Board.

Dale W. Cross is director, Metropolitan Evangelism Strategy, Home Mission Board.

Francis M. DuBose is professor of missions, Golden Gate Baptist Theological Seminary, Mill Valley, California.

Paul N. Geisel is professor, Institute of Urban Studies, University of Texas at Arlington, Arlington, Texas.

C. Kirk Hadaway is research director, Center for Urban Church Studies, Nashville, Tennessee.

Don E. Hammer is director, Metropolitan Missions Department, Home Mission Board.

Larry L. McSwain is professor of church and community, The Southern Baptist Theological Seminary.

Orrin D. Morris is director, Research Division, Home Mission Board.

William M. Pinson, Jr., is president, Golden Gate Baptist Theological Seminary.

Larry L. Rose is executive director, Center for Urban Church Studies.